Kept Secret

Kept Secret

THE HALF-TRUTH IN NONFICTION

Edited by Jen Hirt *and* Tina Mitchell

MICHIGAN STATE UNIVERSITY PRESS | *East Lansing*

⊚ The paper used in this publication meets the minimum requirements
of ANSI/NISO Z39.48-1992 (R 1997) (Permanence of Paper).

Michigan State University Press
East Lansing, Michigan 48823-5245

Printed and bound in the United States of America.

26   25   24   23   22   21   20   19   18   17   1   2   3   4   5   6   7   8   9   10

LIBRARY OF CONGRESS CATALOGING-IN-PUBLICATION DATA
Names: Hirt, Jen, 1975– editor. | Mitchell, Tina, 1978– editor.
Title: Kept secret : the half-truth in nonfiction / edited by Jen Hirt and Tina Mitchell.
Description: East Lansing : Michigan State University Press, 2017.
| Includes bibliographical references.
Identifiers: LCCN 2016028109| ISBN 9781611862478 (pbk. : alk. paper)
| ISBN 9781609175290 (pdf) | ISBN 9781628952995 (epub)
| ISBN 9781628962994 (kindle)
Subjects: LCSH: American essays—21st century. | Creative nonfiction.
| Authors—Interviews. | Secrets.
Classification: LCC PS689 .K47 2017 | DDC 814/.6—dc23
LC record available at https://lccn.loc.gov/2016028109

Book design by Charlie Sharp, Sharp Des!gns, East Lansing, Michigan
Cover design by Shaun Allshouse, www.shaunallshouse.com

Michigan State University Press is a member of the Green Press Initiative and is
committed to developing and encouraging ecologically responsible publishing
practices. For more information about the Green Press Initiative and the use
of recycled paper in book publishing, please visit *www.greenpressinitiative.org.*

Visit Michigan State University Press at *www.msupress.org*

. . .

To Paul and Iván
and everyone who knows
the art of the secret

. . .

There are two kinds of secrets: Those we keep from others, and those we hide from ourselves.

FRANK WARREN, *PostSecret*

One secret is liable to be revealed in the place of another that is harder to tell, and the substitute secret when nakedly exposed is often the more appealing.

EUDORA WELTY, *One Writer's Beginnings*

Contents

Introduction

THE FIRST TIME THE PHRASE "KEPT SECRET" APPEARED IN PRINT WAS IN A fifteenth-century French novel about knights and romance and chivalry. It referenced a passion-filled relationship that was, obviously, a secret kept from friends and enemies. That trend continued for centuries, through plays and poems and prose. And even today, it is the category of love—adultery, crushes, stolen kisses, one-night stands, illicit lovers—that often comes to mind when someone mentions keeping a secret. Take for example *PostSecret*, Frank Warren's 2005 compilation of hundreds of anonymous postcards that each revealed a secret. Many were about love, unrequited relationships, or fetishes.

How interesting, then, that only a handful of the essays in this anthology mention desire or sexual relations as the source of the secret, and both whisper around the elements of shame, not true love. Samuel Autman's "Invisible Nails" narrates his coming out under the judgment of a religion pressuring a conversion from homosexuality. Robin Hemley's "Reading History to My Mother" is about his mother's sudden revelation, late in life, of a rape kept secret for decades. But it's also an essay about Hemley's decision to keep the name of the alleged rapist a secret—authorities (and readers) will never know who did this to his mother.

The rest of the essays have little to do with the traditional topic of secret desire. Is this a trend in creative nonfiction? We think it is. Today's creative nonfiction secrets are more sophisticated and nuanced; they reveal themselves so perfectly via the essay, the genre that is simply "an attempt," as the word originally meant. We think secrets are an attempt to hide what we find shameful, or to become someone we're not, but they are also an attempt to preserve relationships, to deflect grief, to avoid punishment, and to shape perception and thereby reality. They are a way of knowing, and a way of reflecting. Secrets also attempt to solidify a bond between the teller and the keeper. They write their own pact: *If I tell you this, you can't tell anyone.* So what happens, then, when in the course of creative nonfiction's trajectory, writers decide to share their secrets (or parts of those secrets) as widely as possible? Are they still secrets? When someone *tells* a secret, does it get woven into the larger fabric of oral history?

The historian Joan M. Jensen answers "yes" to that last question in "Telling Stories: Keeping Secrets," an article about the struggle historians face in getting rural farm women to reveal secrets in oral history projects. Jensen observes, "Storytelling, and its more modern equivalent oral history, is an old tradition. So, too, is keeping secrets. As historians, our job is to tell stories and to tell secrets. The problem is how to decide which stories to tell and which secrets to keep. Which stories become ours to tell? Which must remain secret?"[1]

The question of "which stories become ours to tell" is one creative nonfiction writers wrestle with constantly. Some of the essays in this collection avoid that problem simply because the writer is revealing his or her own secret—it's always been the writer's secret to tell. Others, however, reveal someone else's secret. And some keep the secret. When a secret is kept, or an open secret is not discussed, can we hear the silence ring half-true? Or do psychic blind spots truly keep us from seeing the elephant in the room?

Questions like these, all on the compelling status of the secret in nonfiction today, got us thinking—what if there were an anthology where each essay contained secrets, lies, or half-truths? Adding to our intrigue was the idea that secrets can keep us from the truth, the foundation on which creative nonfiction is built, no matter how precarious that foundation may be. Here we cross paths with oral historians, who are often recording stories (and secrets) told by the

---

1. Joan M. Jensen, "Telling Stories: Keeping Secrets," *Agricultural History* 83, no. 4 (Fall 2009): 437–45.

displaced, the downtrodden, and the oppressed. Many oral historians do this as an antidote against "the official" version of history; others do it to preserve all histories.

Keeping the idea of oral histories, secrets, and the art of creative nonfiction in mind, we think it is time for creative nonfiction writers to embrace the other, even older connotation of the Old French *essai* ("to try"), which is the connotation of "trial."[2] In a legal trial, a lawyer, like a writer, weighs probabilities to test and ascertain many sides of the same story. And like jurors, readers return a verdict. Commenting on her essay "Leaving Duck Creek," Mary Clearman Blew explains, "The nonfiction writer searches the time capsule for clues like a detective in a crowd of criminals and then describes for her readers what she knows and what she suspects." Through this detective work, the writer is able to get to the heart, or the truth, of the essay. While the truth may inspire us to make confident statements and proclamations, secrets, lies, and half-truths inspire us to hunker down and look harder for clues in the corners where no one else is looking. Eventually, we find what we're after.

Secrets inspire not just content, but also craft. This unique and shared experience can take any form—from humorous to shocking, from lyrical to researched, from brief to epic. As editors, we wanted to showcase this range, because just as we know that people keep secrets for a myriad of reasons, so too will they need a myriad of prose structures as examples for how to tell a secret. Thus, for over a year, we scouted the literary magazines for this theme and its variations on style. We solicited the equivalents of literary troublemakers and trespassers who had a secret. In addition to the essays, we convinced contributors to answer questions about the craft and ethics of secrets in true stories, which often led authors to reveal more secrets they had stashed in a backpack. Or in some cases, like Jo Ann Beard's interview, she playfully keeps the secret.

The word "secret" comes from the Latin *sēcrētus*, meaning to separate or divide. A secret is something we split off from our normal day-to-day interactions.

---

2. The commonplace meaning of "essay"—a short piece of writing on a particular subject—obscures its original meaning as a kind of critical assessment, judgment, or test. Etymologically, "essay," a variant of the Middle English (and modern) "assay" (from the Old French "assai," a test of, or a testing, also the merit of something or someone), goes back to the Latin noun "exagium," which means "weighing" and the verb "exigere," which means "to ascertain or weigh," according to the *Oxford American Dictionary*.

We divide the world into who knows and who does not. We weigh the consequences of revealing the secret. How will the revelation separate us from those who did not know but now know? We also frame secrets, as well as half-truths, with ways of telling. In "Three Takes on a Jump," Jill Christman shows us the three ways to tell a family story that was never really a secret, but the variations conceal the truth. Through her retelling, she discusses "shareability," the idea that, over time, witnesses corroborate and reorganize information in order to represent a traumatic or startling event in a form that is easier to share. As Christman explains in her interview, "The story we think we know has more to do with the telling, and retelling, than it does with memory."

In contrast to the story constructed through shared memory, which becomes the collective memory unless someone questions it as Christman has done, Jo Ann Beard questions her own memory. In "Maybe It Happened," Beard shares a foundational moment of her childhood with a carefully planned repetition of "maybe," "it's possible," "perhaps," and "it's likely." She does this because memory is fallible, and the memory of secrets is dangerously fallible. Everything is a half-truth. She knows the language of half-truth and teaches it to us through her essay.

Beard shows us that even a half-truth can be fully told through creative nonfiction. How is that possible? It's not the revelation of facts that completes an essay; it's the artistry, the *way* it is told, not so much *what* it is telling. Remember that a secret is often whispered. We lower our voices, ask our confidante to lean in, cup our hands to cover the space between lip and ear. Or we close the door, or invite the friend for a walk outside, or say "I'll tell you, later when we're alone." This is where creative nonfiction secret-sharing departs from the secrets revealed in oral histories. Historians might attempt to amplify the secret they've gleaned from an interviewee. Essayists might attempt to keep an element of the whisper.

Given our faulty memories and our love of style, some essayists are moving toward the designation of "free memoir" or "free essay," like "free verse," which defines creative nonfiction that is free to borrow (sometimes quite liberally) from the rules of fiction in order to fill in the gaps of accurate memory. Other writers are prefacing their memoirs with introductions that make it clear what is true and what is exaggerated and what, in some cases, was actually made up. Many readers would likely be wildly disappointed if some of the writers in this collection believed the "creative" aspect of "nonfiction" gave them license to *create* secrets rather than *shape* secrets.

Perhaps it is ironic, then, that beyond the text, a secret can only be a secret if it is *created*, whether that be an individual consciously labeling something as a "secret," or whether it be social and political institutions invoking grand narratives that naturalize social norms and force "others" to live in a state of repression and secrecy, or face persecution. In either case, it takes a brave writer to untangle the knot between the personal, historical, and institutional and get at the truth, as we see in all the essays in this collection. In writing about secrets, these writers illustrate the democratic nature of creative nonfiction and help us have a richer, more inclusive history.

But inclusion, of course, is gendered. In "'Oh, No! It Would Not Be Proper to Discuss That with You': Reflections on Gender and the Experience of Childhood," historian Jean Barman argues that when adults are interviewed by ethnographers in order to reveal long-held stories and secrets from childhood, there is a significant difference in how men tell their stories compared to how women tell their stories. Men, says Barman, will cast themselves as the main actor in the story. Women, in comparison, will frame their stories "within the context of others." Barman concludes with advice for ethnographers and researchers who use the methodology of oral histories: "To understand the childhood of a single person, we must understand both the culture that he or she experienced as a child and the culture perceived as existing at the time that the individual is sharing his or her experience of childhood."[3]

Skilled writers of creative nonfiction figured this out long ago—understanding our childhood secrets requires us to have the ability to write two things: the narrative about the long-ago childhood as well as present-day reflection, interpretation, and insight. But unlike the female participants in Barman's project (many of whom were reluctant to share information because they were overwhelmed by the strictures of social norms), the female writers in this collection have long seen those social norms from the inside and the outside, and as accomplished writers, they provide vivid examples of how to understand dual

---

3. Jean Barman, "'Oh, No! It Would Not Be Proper to Discuss That with You': Reflections on Gender and the Experience of Childhood," *Curriculum Inquiry* 24, no. 1 (Spring 1994): 53–67. Barman conducted her research within a larger project, the Canadian Childhood History Project, which sought, in part, autobiographies written by children about their immediate childhood. She also interviewed adults regarding their private school educations in Canada, which is where she noticed the gendered retelling difference.

cultures—the one in which the secret originally existed, and the one in which they reveal the secret, in an essay, to readers. Leslie Jamison's award-winning essay "The Empathy Exams" is a perfect example.

There is much to be gained by considering creative nonfiction as historical artifact, and students and practitioners of the genre are not surprised that creative nonfiction so easily makes its way into fields outside of literature, including history, sociology, anthropology, psychology, and all the branches therein imbricated with cultural studies. Yet there is a risk in categorizing literary nonfiction as history, which is perhaps what has helped fuel recent trends that push the boundaries of nonfiction a bit harder than writers in the recent past. Essays are highly crafted art objects that belong in the realm of literature *and* history. In this light, then, it is important to consider that the analysis of historical objects requires different approaches, especially when concerning secrets.

We hope, then, that readers will like how we're adding stylistic branches in the evolutionary tree of creative nonfiction. Essays about secrets, lies, and half-truths encourage both writers and readers to unlock the secret of the text. But why not also go to the source, and see the writers unlocking the craft of their secrets? That is why we've included a short interview for each selection. We're letting the interviews, not labels, provide clarity into the levels of half-truth in these essays. Through the interviews, readers are better able to hear authorial intention. The interviews also instruct writers of all levels on how to write about their own detective work in uncovering a secret (or constructing a half-truth in order to keep one).

The consequences of revealing secrets is another problematic aspect. Amy E. Robillard's "Changing the Subject" deftly handles parallel mother-daughter secrets. Ron Tanner's "My Father's Secrets" gives voice to a father whose secret he was contractually obliged not to reveal. The secret keeper is not the only person affected by the secret; families and friends and coworkers fall into the secret's gravitational field. So where are the ethical boundaries? In "Secret Machine," Brenda Miller limns the boundary as she stands in the studio of an artist trying to process the collapsing hours of September 11, an artist who can barely speak aloud what her work seems to make obvious to strangers. Miller decides to tell this artist's story, and in essence tell her secret; in the interview, Miller explains the complexities of 9/11 secrets, especially when they are not yours. She is sensitive to timing: when do you say what you need to say?

And how do you put into words the secrets about death and violence? For Jon Pineda, it's the lyrical fragmented essay that proves most useful. He takes us on the s-turns (a surfing term) of his sister's untimely death. In "Okay Forever," Barrett Swanson scours a surveillance tape for what secrets it reveals about his brother's traumatic brain injury suffered outside a bar one night. Pineda's essay is brief; Swanson's is an extended narrative. Both forms succeed.

We also have essays about smaller secrets, the proverbial white lies, headed up by Erin Murphy's flash nonfiction piece appropriately titled "White Lies," where a classmate's lie does more good than harm. And while most essays about secrets are sobering, even hard to read due to the content, Kelly Kathleen Ferguson shows us how to be hilarious with an absurd lie in another school essay, the amusing "Experiments in Living Chemistry." What Ferguson puts in her Petri dish and what she says is in the Petri dish makes for an epic situation.

We close the anthology with Sarah Gorham's "On Lying" with its Montaigne-themed title. She frames her discussion about lying and art with a story about the time she lied to her daughter's teacher just for the ease of a family vacation—but of course it's much more than that.

We hope that this anthology serves as a guide and a resource, as well as just good reading from talented writers. With so many flat-out fraudulent memoirs getting attention, there is a need for transparency behind the process of how we tell our truths and how we tell our secrets. If even only one of these interviews helps a writer decide how to share an important secret with an audience, then we feel that *Kept Secret* will have succeeded.

Maybe It Happened

Jo Ann Beard

MAYBE SHE WAS A KID. MAYBE SHE WASN'T QUITE HOUSEBROKEN. MAYBE SHE was playing outside one summer afternoon with a couple of older cousins who were. Maybe they got deeply involved in a game where she was the baby and they were taking care of her. Maybe this involved cooing and being pushed in a wagon and having bows tied into her slippery, nonexistent hair. Maybe when the moment came that the baby should have gotten up out of the wagon and excused herself to go indoors and use the facilities, the baby decided instead to really get into her role. Maybe she wet her pants.

It's possible the oldest of the older cousins was nine, and possible that the youngest of the older cousins was seven. It's possible that the nine-year-old wore a fashion-conscious sherbet-orange skirt and a ruffled midriff top, making her seem even more sophisticated than her actual years, and possible that the other one wore a sleeveless white blouse, gray pleated shorts, and glasses with light blue frames, making her seem like a seven-year-old teacher. It's possible that they were bored, stuck at somebody else's house for the afternoon with nothing to play with except a little kid who had just sat there and peed while they were petting her, like a puppy. It's possible that they abandoned playing mothers then, to go sit on the stoop and squint into the summer sunlight, waiting to have their

1

pictures taken so they could be seen many years later as they looked that day, hugging their knees, silently sharing their pop-bead wardrobe, one wearing the bracelet, the other wearing the necklace.

Perhaps the baby who wasn't a baby climbed up on a metal milk crate like they used to have back then and peered through the back window at her mother and her aunt. Perhaps her mother was sitting at the kitchen table with her head stuck through a plastic tablecloth, drinking coffee from one of the pink Melmac cups that would outlast all the people in this story, and all the people reading this story. Perhaps the mother was smoking a cigarette and was holding it out every so often so that the aunt, who was wearing plastic gloves and mixing up a vat of hair dye, could take drags off it. Perhaps the flat bottle of liquor that the mother and this particular aunt favored was sitting on the table. Perhaps they had dosed their coffee with it, in order not to "kill the children." Perhaps just beyond them was the small, neat living room, with its chunky green furniture and its cabbage-rose draperies closed against the sun. Perhaps all the way through, nearly to the front door, was their telephone table, on which sat the heavy black telephone with a dial that the kid in soggy shorts standing on the metal milk box could barely even move. Perhaps the mother herself resorted to using a stubby pencil to dial this phone, which suddenly rang out in the tiny house, a loud, old-fashioned sound, startling everyone and causing the milk box to wobble and the mother, who was getting her head painted dark brown, to say "Shit" in a loud voice.

It's likely then that the tipped milk box pitched its rider onto the dirt by the back door, embedding a piece of gravel in her right knee, leaving a pale blue O-shaped spot that, along with two accommodating moles, would form what she would ever after think of as that knee's stricken face. It's likely as well that the mother, wearing her plastic tablecloth poncho, walked through the living room with its one dramatic dark green wall to the telephone. Just as likely is that the aunt stayed where she was, setting down the bowl of dye and whatever she was applying it with, which is why while the mother was picking up the phone and saying hello and then listening to what the caller had to say, the aunt was peeling off the gloves and stepping out onto the back stoop to pick up the kid who had fallen onto a sharp rock and was wailing. It's likely the aunt was confused for a long moment that afternoon, about why when she got the soggy child with the bloody knee calmed down, she still heard crying.

Or did she? Maybe on those hot summer afternoons, when coffee made women languid, when the scent of trellis roses mixed with the scent of ammonia, when girls pretended they were mothers while mother pretended something else entirely, perhaps anything could happen.

But then again, it's maybe possible, perhaps likely, that it never did.

Interview with Jo Ann Beard

1. This piece first appeared in *O, the Oprah Magazine* in 2008, a couple of years after Oprah's confrontation with writer James Frey, who had fabricated part of his memoir. Was the Frey scandal on your mind as you wrote this? Did anyone at *O, the Oprah Magazine* try to fact-check your piece? As a writer whose work has been celebrated for how it falls between nonfiction and fiction, how do you decide what is ethical to cast as half-truth, and what (if anything) has to adhere to full truth?

James Frey was very much on my mind when I was writing the piece—I didn't agree to do it, but only agreed to try to do it, because sometimes the writing goes its own way and tries to make something interesting out of something that isn't. Like peeing one's pants at an age when it's almost acceptable to do so. I stalled for days and weeks; everything that I wrote had untruths in it—how did I know what I was wearing, what kind of cup my mother was drinking out of, what my cousins were thinking, etc.?—the kinds of questions that are meaningless in memoir, of course, but still I was stuck back in that moment, standing in the doorway of my living room watching through my fingers as poor James Frey was publicly shamed for the benefit of the studio audience and all of us at home. You would think he had lied about weapons of mass destruction instead of exaggerating his own self-destruction. I don't believe anyone fact-checked my essay at *O*, because the editorial staff at *O* is more sophisticated than that; how do you fact-check something that is purely speculative? There probably is no such thing as a half-truth, and the full truth is subject to the particular sensibility it's being filtered through. That goes for essays, for magazine articles, and for newspapers. I know certain facts about my own experiences, as well as anyone can, but facts are not what make a memoir live and breathe. What gives life to memoir are the physical details and the emotions and the words that were spoken—sometimes remembered and sometimes imagined—and the meaning that is made of all those things together.

2. Your first paragraph's sentences start with "Maybe." Second paragraph, "It's possible." Third, "Perhaps." And the last paragraph has "It's likely." This wording emphasizes uncertainty. Why should writers embrace uncertainty?

Well, the easy answer is that life is uncertain, memory is unreliable, and the truth is malleable. But in fact, I was just playing around. To me as writer, the fun part was skirting the issue of truth-in-memoir by using those words and then getting to figure out how to fashion a final sentence that had all of them in there. So finally the assignment felt engaging instead of intimidating, and in an hour I had finished the piece and liked it.

3. We never find out the nature of the phone call, although we know it is bad news. The full details are literally kept secret from the reader, because the piece ends. Why did you decide to end it like that? Have any readers ever asked you what the phone call was about?

Nobody has ever asked that question, but then again, nobody has ever mentioned that essay to me until now. In my own mind, the phone call is probably the most important thing in the essay, but the mystery is what makes that so.

4. Does the girl, as an adult, still have a scar? And how are scars like secrets?

If the girl ever had that scar, I believe she would still have it now. Since she rarely lets people see her knees, it's hard to say. Even though she writes memoir, she keeps her scars secret.

My Father's Secrets

Ron Tanner

WHEN I WAS FOURTEEN AND FIFTEEN, I LIVED WITH MY FAMILY ON A SMALL
island called Kwajalein, part of an atoll with the same name, in the middle of
the Pacific Ocean. It was, and still is, a top-secret missile test site for the U.S.
Army. Now called the Ronald Reagan Ballistic Missile Defense Test Site, the
atoll possesses one of the largest arrays of radar antennas in the world. One of
them, called the ALTAIR, is as big as a baseball diamond and looms from the
equatorial jungle like something from a James Bond movie—a giant laser that's
capable, say, of blowing up the moon. It is, in fact, sensitive enough to track a
wrench floating from a space shuttle. My father worked at the ALTAIR site, on
an island near Kwajalein.

He called himself an "electrical engineer," but this wasn't entirely accurate.
You have to have top-level security clearance to work at facilities like ALTAIR.
That's why my father never answered the question *What do you do for work,
Daddy?* He was sworn to secrecy. By the time our family moved to Kwajalein, I
had given up asking him such questions. At first, it seemed he wasn't articulate
enough to explain his work—he was a shy man—but then, as I kept asking over
the years, it became clear he was hiding something. He wasn't a dishonest man—I

knew that much—but I wondered why he quietly refused to give me what most fathers would have happily offered.

The sum total I knew of my father's history I could have written on a postcard. He was the only child of a feckless, alcoholic father and a tough Appalachian mother, both of whom labored in California's orange groves and packing houses. In 1942, at age seventeen, he joined the Navy and then saw three years of fighting in the Pacific. As a child, I often dug through his steamer trunks in our basement and pored over the artifacts that told of his life as a young man. There was a Japanese officer's sword, a hara-kiri knife, Navy medals, old foreign coins, mothballed uniforms, old photos, a couple of high school yearbooks, even artwork he'd done as a schoolboy. I found several yellowed photos of him in his Navy whites, always smiling. He had a great smile, which my mother says I inherited. One snapshot showed him grinning with a grass-skirted hula dancer in Honolulu. He was a radio operator on a Navy cruiser. By the time he sailed west toward Japan, his ship would have been in contact with the top-secret long-range radio facility (constructed in 1943) in the Koolau Mountains on the island of Oahu, not far from Pearl Harbor. That is to say, his life of secrets began early—six years before he met the young woman who would become my mother.

Although my father had an obvious aptitude for electronics, he really wanted to be a farmer, and, in fact, he tried his hand at raising cucumbers in California after the war. The crop failed, and he never ate another cucumber for the rest of his life. Four years later, after earning a degree in engineering, he was recruited by Western Electric, a company that worked with Bell Laboratories to do research and development for the U.S. military. My mother told me he helped test one of the first nuclear-powered submarines, though it was an assignment I could never verify since it was shrouded in secrecy. Years later, while at work on other secret projects, my father wore a wallet-sized badge that measured the level of radiation he was exposed to. My mother told me his badge was tested every month to make sure he wasn't overexposed. "It was bullshit," she says now of this precaution. "He was so irradiated, he should have glowed in the dark." When he died of stomach cancer at forty-nine, she blamed overexposure to electromagnetic radiation.

But I knew none of this when I was a teenager living on that secret missile base in the middle of the Pacific. It would be decades before I learned that my father's specialty was radars and their antennas. One afternoon, out of boredom—of which there was an abundance on our island—I decided to climb an antenna at the south end of Kwajalein. The antenna was a semicircular steel grid forty feet high. I was good at climbing, and the structure's fretwork made it easy. Within a short time, I was twenty feet off the ground. That's when a security guard showed up.

"Get down from there," he called. "You'll kill yourself."

I looked down at him, a middle-aged man with few prospects. "It's my life," I called. "What do you care?"

"You get down from there right now!" he shouted, swiping his fist at the air. I didn't understand why he was so upset. When I touched ground, he dragged me to his pickup truck and drove me to the police station. It just so happened that my mother was at the sergeant's desk, renewing her bicycle license. Even though I was often getting dragged to the police station, my mother, who retained an astoundingly resilient naiveté, was surprised to see me.

"I don't understand," she said. "Why aren't you in school?"

It occurs to me now that had I reached the top of the antenna, I might have been too weary to climb down. Fatigued, I might have lost my grip and fallen. How ironic would that have been, to have accidentally killed myself on the very thing to which my father had dedicated his life?

I was often getting into trouble on Kwajalein. Mostly, I'd sneak out to drink beer with friends. Beer was easy to get. If you didn't steal it, as my best friend Spud did, you could buy it from vending machines at Bachelor's Beach for a quarter a can. In the tropics, it was summer year round, and we wayward teens had a blast running through Kwajalein's leafy alleys after curfew, when the grown-ups were sleeping. We did this nearly every weekend. One night, Spud downed sixteen beers and got so drunk I nearly had to carry him home.

His arm slung over my shoulder, I struggled to keep him upright and moving. It seemed he could say nothing more than "Fucking-A, man!"

Fortunately, we didn't have far to walk because it was such a small island, but we had to be mindful of Security, the civilian rent-a-cops who acted as our police force. We teens despised Security. They drove slowly through the neighborhoods in white pickups, their spotlights scanning the nooks and crannies, roofs, and patios for curfew breakers.

Dogs were prohibited on Kwajalein, so it was quiet but for the clatter of palm fronds in the breeze overhead and the distant wash of waves. I was dizzy from my beers, but I wasn't drunk. Spud's house was a little larger than mine because his father was higher up in the hierarchy, but his furniture was made of Japanese bamboo like ours—like everybody's. Inside, I could smell the stink of the cigars

Spud's father smoked. Spud stumbled then fell to the linoleum floor. He started cursing. I motioned for him to be quiet.

Then he looked up at me, grinned, and said, "Fucking-A!"

Suddenly, the room brightened. Someone had flicked on the overhead light. Spud's father, wearing a bathrobe and slippers, stood in the hallway that led to the house's three small bedrooms. I expected him to have a cigar in one hand, as it seemed he always did. He was a pugnacious little man, with an underbite and small eyes. I saw something of Spud in his face. He said, "What're you boys doing?"

I winced at the light and said, "I brought Spud home."

"What'd you do to him?" He stared in disbelief at his son, who was still sprawled on the floor. "You been drinking?"

"Dad?" Spud propped himself on one elbow and looked up at his father. He could hardly talk. "Dad?"

It sounded like he was asking for something—sympathy? help? forgiveness?

Spud's father stared at his boy in pained disbelief. Then he glared at me. I wanted to protest: *I've brought my friend home. I've looked after him. I did not get Spud drunk!* But I was not practiced at talking back, and I felt bad about Spud.

His father said, "You get out of here."

My face burning, I walked out. When I stepped into my house minutes later, our cat pushed between my ankles and squeaked a greeting. Spud was going to be OK, I told myself. And we had escaped Security, hadn't we? That was something to be proud of. And I had handled my liquor, hadn't I? I was growing up, I decided. I made myself a ham sandwich. Then the phone rang, startling me. I answered quickly, thinking it would be Spud. Or his father.

The caller identified himself as a Security officer. He asked if I'd been out drinking. I hesitated to answer. He said, "Come on, I know you have. Just tell me the truth."

"If I tell you the truth," I said, "will you tell my parents?"

"I just want to know if you've been out tonight." He spoke casually, like a friend.

"You won't tell my parents?" I asked.

"No," he said easily, "just tell me if you've been out."

"Yes," I said. "I've been out."

"Drinking?"

"Yes."

After a pause, he said, just as easily as before, "Let me speak to your father."

"Why?"

"I just want to talk to him for a minute."

"He's sleeping," I said.

"That's all right. You can wake him up."

Again, I hesitated, then asked, "Are you going to tell him what I said?"

"No, I'm not. Just let me speak to him."

I padded upstairs. I was barefoot, as always. I eased open the door of my parents' bedroom. I seldom entered their room. The grown-up smells—Dad's spice cologne, Mom's perfume, the warm bedclothes-heated otherness of their bodies—I found interesting and intimidating.

When I touched my father's shoulder, he rose slightly and said, "What's wrong?" as if he were ready to take my temperature or get me medicine. It occurred to me that I was not far removed from being a little boy.

"Someone's on the phone. He wants to talk to you."

My father was tall and lanky, a good-looking man. He had started taking scuba lessons and was suntanned and sinewy. As he followed me downstairs, he asked, "Who?" He was wearing boxers and a white T-shirt.

"It's a Security officer. He wants to talk to you." My heart was pulsing at the back of my tongue. But I was safe, I reminded myself. The officer had given me his promise.

Now, my mother was behind us. "What is it?" She was wearing a full slip.

Downstairs, the three of us stood in our small kitchen. I watched my father, receiver to his ear, listening intently to the Security officer. Then my father looked down at me and said, "Did you sneak out tonight? This man says you went drinking."

"Drinking!" my mother echoed.

I shook my head in firm denial. "No, I didn't!"

My father nodded his satisfaction, then said into the phone, "My son tells me he didn't go out tonight. You must be mistaken."

My father listened some more. He looked perplexed. Then he held the receiver away from his ear as if it was suddenly very hot. He narrowed his eyes at me. "He says you told him you *did* go out. Did you?"

I felt my face burning. I saw my mother watching as if she had just witnessed a car crash. I said, "Yeah, I did."

Then something happened to my father's face. He paled and almost winced.

It was like watching an avalanche, like seeing some part of him fall into himself, and I knew I had betrayed him, had hurt him in ways I couldn't begin to undo.

I would spend years trying to make this up to him, even as I continued to hurt and disappoint him.

After we moved back to the States, my father attached a massive motorized antenna to the side of our house. It extended ten feet above the roof. A brown plastic dial atop our television set, in the den, allowed us to direct the antenna to any point on the compass and thus receive good reception. When I was growing up in the 1960s, an antenna—whether on the head of a cartoon robot, the rear of an automobile, or the barrel of a toy ray gun—was considered a cool thing. An antenna put you "out there," connecting you to something beyond yourself; it was about power and reach. That's what made antennas scary when Martians sprouted them. That's what made them sexy when extended from portable radios. And that's why it was a point of pride for men like my father to talk about TV antennas—how good theirs were, how many channels theirs pulled in. An antenna was a metallic finger held up to the electromagnetic wind. It gave you a read on the world. If you didn't have one, you were, literally, "out of it."

When TV went digital in 2009, I refused to get cable and, instead, decided to plant an antenna on our roof. A profound dislike of the cable company's monopoly informed my decision, but so did a sentimental attraction to the old technology that had been central to my father's life.

An antenna is nothing more than a crude metal net erected to catch the messy wash of electromagnetic waves spilling over the earth's surface—signals generated by cell phones, computers, radios, televisions, electric garage doors, virtually any electrical apparatus, but most especially remote-control devices, and, of course, the ever-flaring sun. Sometimes, in this soup of radio waves, a rogue signal will cause an automated garage door to open seemingly by itself. Such a sight may surprise or even startle us, but really it shouldn't. We are immersed in radio waves every minute of our lives: they saturate the air we breathe.

It may occur to you, as it has to many, that this random, profligate wash of radio waves should be cause for worry, if not alarm. The International Conference on Cell Tower Siting expressed concern about potentially carcinogenic cell phone radiation as early as 2000. Four years before that, the FCC established a radiation limit for phones. To test radio wave penetration, technicians immerse a probe inside a liquid-filled dummy that replicates a human's aqueous body. The probe measures how the waves of a nearby cell phone resonate through the dummy. As it happens, our bodies make marvelous antennas. If the thought of radio waves roiling through your inner sea gives you pause, then you are not alone. Surely my father considered the risks involved in his work, surrounded by machines that sliced and diced his body with their rays. Electrical engineers of his caliber were more than aware of these things.

The word *antenna* was used first in Latin, as a nautical term to signify "that which goes before," specifically the "sail yard" of a ship. The Greek equivalent of this term describes the appendages at the forefront of an insect, generally referred to as "horns." Whether on a ship or an insect, they are "foremost"—the thing we see first, which is why we associate antennas with sentinel duty and warning, even alarm.

SCR-270, a mobile radar that was supposed to guard Pearl Harbor in 1941, was a fairly simple device, though advanced for its time. It sent short bursts of high-frequency signals into the atmosphere. If any of these hit a metallic object within a hundred and fifty miles, that signal would bounce back to the radar's antenna. The radar technician could determine the position of the interfering object by calculating the duration of the signal's return. The more signals that bounced back, the more cause there was for concern. On December 7, 1941, the antenna was stationed at the northernmost tip of Oahu, thirty miles from Pearl Harbor.

At 7:02 that morning, shortly before shutting down the antenna per orders (since there was apparently nothing to watch), the primary technician, Private Joseph L. Lockard, was showing his trainee, Private George Elliott, how to improve his abilities to read the radar screen. Elliott recounts, "Suddenly there appeared the largest blip either of us had seen on an oscilloscope." They checked the scope and determined it was working properly. The mass of interference was 137 miles northeast and growing nearer.

When Elliott and Lockard phoned their base to report the massive reading on their oscilloscope, the commanding lieutenant told them that it was, without question, a dozen B-17 Flying Fortresses scheduled to arrive that morning from San Francisco. (We may wonder now: did the Japanese know of the expected B-17s and dummy an early arrival?) Assured that theirs was a false alarm, Elliott and Lockard continued their watch—now as recreation. They tracked the oncoming planes until they were only twenty-two miles away, at which point nearby mountains obscured their approach to Pearl Harbor.

Less than a year later, Lockard and Elliot were called to the steps of the U.S. Capitol to receive medals for having done their duty on that infamous day. Lockard received the Distinguished Service Medal. Elliot was to be given the Legion of Merit but refused it, insisting he should get no less than Lockard. Elliot died at eighty-five of a stroke in 2003; the *Los Angeles Times* obit focused on the missed opportunity that haunted him till the end of his life. His son said, "He had a feeling of frustration that if the warning had been heeded, they could have at least got planes in the air and lives could have been saved."

In 2009, the television antenna setup my wife and I bought at a retro electronics store was surprisingly complicated. I had envisioned nothing more than a modest metallic sprout planted on the roof, but it demanded strapping the antenna to the chimney, running a line into the house, and running a cable to a lightning rod in the backyard. No wonder the cable companies were immediately and immensely popular when they offered an affordable alternative in the 1970s. Suddenly, the antenna was uncool—a kitschy throwback, the kind of thing you'd see on grandma's house. Even car manufacturers started hiding them. The irony of the cable revolution was that it made us think our antennas were obsolete when they weren't. The truth is, we simply moved the antennas to the cable companies, and the cable companies, in turn, sent us the transmissions via their cables.

Our new antenna came in a big cardboard box that reminded me of a construction set I had gotten for Christmas long ago. Made of aluminum, it was folded up like a logic puzzle—a bristly array of aluminum rods and fins that must be turned and snapped into place—and immediately I was anxious I might not figure it out. When I finally had the thing put together, it extended six feet across and looked like the *Voyager I* space probe. Then I recalled that *Voyager I*, launched in 1977, is still "out there." It takes NASA eighteen hours to contact this now-crude but remarkable space probe, which was supposed to function for only four years but has continued transmitting and has recently left our solar system, from whose misty borders our sun looks 1/10,000 as bright as it does here on Earth.

If I hooked a powerful radio receiver to our new antenna, I could hear transmissions from deep space. There is plenty to hear, apparently, though mostly it's just the static of the stars. So far, there's nothing "artificial"—that is, nothing created by sentient beings. Still, scientists say it's only a matter of time, because given that there are hundreds of billions of planets in the inner galactic plane to survey, it's likely that there's a planet or two of thinking creatures who are sending signals of some sort. As for earthlings who think the deliberate messages we send into outer space only invite our own destruction—starting with the record made of gold on *Voyager 1*, which includes whale songs and the sound of the wind, as well as Navajo night chants and samples of Bach concertos—it's too late. "The fact is, for better or for worse, we have already announced our presence and location to the universe, and continue to do so every day," astronomer Carl Sagan reminded us decades ago. "There is a sphere of radio transmission about thirty light years thick expanding outward at the speed of light, announcing to every star it envelops that the earth is full of people. Our television programs flood space with signals detectable at enormous distances by instruments not much greater than our own. It is a sobering thought that the first news of us may be the outcome of the Super Bowl."

After my arrest for drinking and breaking curfew on yet another night on Kwajalein, my father came to pick me up at the police station. He was now used to this routine. I was fifteen, and it wasn't clear to either of us what might become of me. When he walked into the station, he looked neither disappointed nor angry. He simply said, "Let's go," and I followed him outside to his bicycle. There was no bicycle for me, so I had to run behind him. "Keep up," he said.

Half-drunk and barefoot, I ran, grateful for this modest humiliation—it was a message I could easily understand. Once we got home, my father said, "Go to bed." And that was all he said about the incident. The next morning, as I held my aching head and stared at my breakfast cereal, my mother told me I was grounded for a month. My father had long gone to work. When he returned that night, wearing the uniform of his geeky tribe (Bermuda shorts, black knee socks, dress shoes, and a crisp short-sleeved shirt), he offered no lectures, no tirades. I was disappointed because if he had nothing to say now—about his feelings, about his hopes for me—he would never have anything to say.

I hold many memories of my father as a role model, and I understand that, absent his ability to talk to me, this was how he showed his love. One night when I was five, my mother beckoned my brother and me to follow her—quietly—down the hallway of our modest ranch house. There, at the darkened doorway of my parents' bedroom, we peered in and saw my father on his knees, hands folded, eyes closed, praying by the bed he shared with my mother. For years, I prayed like that, too, every night.

My father seemed to know everything about everything. He showed my brother and me how to scavenge through tide pools and low-tide reefs on Kwajalein. He made sure to instruct us to replace the rocks we overturned so we would not harm the habitat (the sun would kill sea life exposed on the bottom of overturned rocks). "Reefing" became my favorite hobby on Kwajalein. I was amazed at the things I came across. One day, I brought home a bomb casing the size of a boot, a relic of World War II. I'd been pounding it clean with a reef rock. When I showed it to my father, he examined it carefully. "See that?" He pointed to the welt in the bull's-eye of the casing bottom. "That's a blasting cap," he said. "You could have blown your hand off."

In our second year on Kwajalein, my mother suggested I accompany my father when he went snorkeling. He was an avid snorkeler and had started an extensive shell collection. One Saturday, in a gesture of camaraderie, I went out with Dad in a Boston Whaler, a tiny motorboat. I didn't much like the water, and that day, I didn't feel like going in, so I waited in the boat while my father dove. At the time, I wasn't yet aware of my sensitivity to motion, but, as the hot day wore on and I sat in the bobbing boat, smelling the fishy reek of coral my father had uprooted and thrown at my feet, I realized with alarm that I was seasick. I didn't want to make a scene or whine to go home, so I toughed it out. But when we got back to Kwajalein, I all but ran home for relief, leaving my father far behind without an explanation. I felt terrible about it and, even then, wished I could have explained myself. My father may have imagined I couldn't wait to get away from him. I doubt he supposed I was incapable of communicating with him because of his unwitting example.

The last time I saw my father, I was a senior in college. It was winter. We were meeting my brother and grandmother to spend a week at a beach house. When I picked my parents up at the airport, I was stunned not only by how ill my father looked—his complexion was gray, he had lost thirty pounds, and he was wearing a hairpiece to hide the effects of chemotherapy—but also by the way he embraced me fervently. He had never done that, and I realized there was more emotion than I knew in this man whom I'd never seen cry. That week, I watched my father trying hard to be a regular guy, going so far as to ignore his medical restrictions so he could have a glass of wine with my brother and me.

Because I strived to be as stoic and self-contained as my father, I sought no counseling and solicited no help from family or friends when he died later that year. As a result, it took me fifteen years to come to terms with my loss. Early on, I kept thinking I saw him passing in a crowd. Once, I nearly chased down a man who looked like my father, but when the stranger turned around to find me behind him, I reared back, suddenly aware he could not possibly be the man my father had been. For years, night after night, I dreamed of searching for my father—often lost in a crowd. When I was lucky enough to find him, we embraced as I wept into his shoulder. I'd wake exhausted, having spent hours in my dream weeping.

My father seemed lost to me, like a satellite spiraling into the deep time of space. I recalled the mysteries of his basement workshop: the handfuls of diodes and transistors, which looked to my childish eyes like penny candy, and the electronic gizmos he used to test distance, sound, and the trajectories of airborne objects. There was an oscilloscope, whose porthole-sized screen showed a bright green, bouncing line that zigged and zagged as magically as an illuminated sprite. Now, in the penumbra of his death, I wondered: had he been a necromancer, a demi-wizard, or just one of so many hapless grunts toiling in the toxic bowels of the military industrial complex? My mother could offer no answers. He had shared with her nearly nothing of his work. I had to wait two decades—until his work was no longer classified—for an answer. Then I phoned one of his former colleagues, now retired. This man knew me and welcomed my call and understood my need to ask so many questions.

I said, "Dad worked on missiles that shot down other missiles. That's all I know."

"In your father's day, we had more time to shoot down an incoming missile than they do now," Mr. Reiger said over the phone. "As much as forty minutes."

I'd first met Mr. Reiger on Kwajalein. Like so many of my father's colleagues, he was smart and a little geeky. I remembered him mostly for his irreverent humor, his eyes glinting with mischief. I was grateful he was willing to talk with me.

"It was like a video game," he continued, "except high stakes. Every missile has a distinct 'signature' we're trying to assess in that time. Well, now the time is down to ten minutes." This made him laugh.

"Ten minutes," I exclaimed. "Jesus."

I was sitting at my desk in my home office. Through my window, a gray scrim of snow made my historic neighborhood look faded, like an old photograph.

"Your father was a systems analyst," he said. "His job involved reentry physics. He came up with algorithms to detect signatures and mass-to-drag ratios—all of the things that help us identify and target the incoming missile."

"In ten minutes."

"That's where the formulas come in. He had to find out if the software was telling the hardware the right things to do. The Roi [ALTAIR] facility collected the data, and we analyzed it."

"In ten minutes."

"Well, we had twenty. The missiles [we fire] have gotten faster, but they haven't gotten much smarter," he said.

"Why not smarter?"

"It's not worth the investment," he said, "given what these missiles do."

"Blow things to smithereens."

"If they can find their targets."

"Do they find the targets?" I asked. "Are they *going* to find their targets?"

"We've been working on this for over forty years with mixed results."

He said this without judgment or emotion, as a scientist might. Maybe that's the attitude these engineers had worked hard to cultivate. They were the best minds in the world, working on one of the most impossible projects. Who could blame them if, ultimately, the challenge was beyond their means?

Outside, I heard a car revving in the icy street, its wheels spinning for traction.

"So the whole Star Wars Strategic Defense Initiative is a failure?" I asked.

"Well, Ron, we're nowhere near developing HEDIs, High Endoatmospheric Defense Interceptors, or even the MSX, Midcourse Space Experiment, and you can forget about the SBI, space-based interceptor. If NASA can barely keep its stations in orbit, how long do you think it's going to take us to perfect satellite warfare?"

Out of respect, I didn't ask the most obvious question, which my mother had been asking ever since my father's death: *then why bother?*

I recalled my father's basement workshop, all the tools he had arrayed neatly on pegboards, and his arcane instruments—electronics testing equipment, black boxes brimming with dials and knobs.

"So," I said, summarizing, "in ten minutes, you've got to find the missile, determine its 'assets,' target it, then shoot it down."

"Don't forget about the decoys," he added.

"There are decoys?"

"Lots of them," he said. "Fired with the real missiles. That's where asset and signature analysis comes in. When your father and I were working on Roi, the shots came at us from the Air Force at Vandenberg, which is about the range that any enemy missile would fire from: nearly five thousand miles."

"Radar is key, obviously."

"That's right, Ron. Radar is key."

Recently, I spent some time in Maine, where I saw many falling stars. One of them was a large blue-green streak, whose abrupt burst blanched the night sky like sheet lightning. It made me yelp in surprised awe. As wondrous and beautiful as they are—or perhaps because they are so wondrous and beautiful—the sight of falling meteors makes me a little sad. Almost always, they remind me of my father, the secretive antenna expert. The irony of his life was that he was a communication specialist who communicated so very little with his sons. He was a good father in all the traditional ways, but a large part of him was, and remains, as mysterious as a falling star. And so whenever I behold a star-stunned night sky, I want to believe that by staring into space, I might somehow reach him or channel something of him back to me. I know this makes no sense.

But that's how our species is. Even if we had proof that it would be madness to send our signals into space, we would probably do it anyway. Hardwired to communicate, we are irrevocably, impulsively communal. I would like to think that even those who seem most uncommunicative, like my father, communicate nevertheless. It's just that they do so in ways we can't quite catch. We attempt to read them the way we attempt to read signals from deep space. To accept this is to accept limits most of us would rather not acknowledge. That's why many people surveying the now-naked rooftops of my neighborhood would see the lone antenna atop our house and scoff, assuming it's as obsolete as the Model T. Perhaps they would change their minds and think more deeply about this—and every—form of communication, if they understood that our lowly aerial is cousin to the *Voyager* space probe, which even now is hurtling through the outer reaches of our solar system and still dutifully, regularly, sending signals home.

Interview with Ron Tanner

1. What was the biggest challenge in writing about your father's secrets, and do you have any advice for writers in similar situations?

Until completing "My Father's Secrets," I had never been able to write successfully about my father, because the topic was both emotionally fraught (he died young) and impenetrable (much of his life was a secret). Only after I put his secrets in the forefront did the topic open up for me. There is still so much about him and his work that I will never know.

It may seem to us essayists—or so it seemed to me—that we must be masters of our material (i.e., we reveal all secrets), but I realized that sometimes it's okay to be clueless. In fact, literary history shows us that cluelessness is at the core of the essay. We essay in order to discover. That's how I approached this essay: what do I know of my father and what might I learn if I try to put some order to this jumble of fragments?

2. Aside from discussing your father's job with his colleague, what was your research process like? What was involved in researching classified work and in turn waiting for it to become declassified?

The hardest part of researching this essay was the fact that my father's colleagues were legally and morally bound by an oath of silence. So, for years, I was pushing at that closed door. Until that door opened, in the early 2000s, I was relegated to interviewing around the topic: what did my mother remember? What did my brother recall? But then the Internet revolution changed everything. By 2004, it seemed everything and everybody had a website—even the top-secret missile base on Kwajalein. I got tons of information from this and other sites. The Internet made secrets impossible to keep. That's when I knew I could call one of my father's colleagues and, finally, ask questions they had refused to answer for decades.

3. After your father's death, you continue to be self-contained, which amplifies your grief. You also explain that humans are hardwired to communicate. In this sense, do you think secrets are unnatural?

We hold secrets at our peril. Secrets run counter to our fundamental nature to share and cooperate. If held too long, secrets will damage, if not destroy, us. The writer's tacit charge—whether as a journalist, a historian, or a poet—is to unveil secrets and, we hope, expose the truth. This is what makes writing so challenging and sometimes seemingly impossible.

Secret Machine

Brenda Miller

My loneliness is a secret machine,
a flying featherbed in the blue
of a hydrangea . . .

—Christopher Howell, "Galileo"

I.

IN TARA PARSONS' MONOTYPES, AIRPLANES FLY AT YOU FROM MANY ANGLES: sometimes head on, or buzzing away, swooping straight into the stratosphere. Sometimes they tilt a bit, as if nodding their wings in your direction, but most often they stay a course away from the center, grazing the edge—a nimbus of white wings and tail, an empty body that punctuates otherwise deep fields of blue. At first glance this blue seems harmless, and the planes themselves oddly cheerful, like stenciled decorations adorning the room of a child: one who wakes happy and calls out for his mother—not in distress, no, but wanting only to share his glee at all the airplanes that greet him.

Tara works all day in her studio, and sometimes at night, cautiously blading the stencils of the same airplane—a toy model of a Continental Airlines jet—and then pulling them through the press to see how they will fly. Sometimes you feel the uplift, and sometimes the breath-catch of touchdown, but most often you're reminded of that pause in the middle of the long flight, a stretch of time when the plane settles in—you feel suspended in that blue, with no clear destination, and you think maybe you'll be up here forever, reading your book, doing the crossword, dozing, waiting for the rattle of the in-flight service cart making its second rounds.

When you see these prints in Tara's studio, hanging from a line by clothespins, you can get a little dizzy: this multitude of jets inching forward, both in motion and deathly still. And you try not to notice that some of these planes startle back, rearing above a black plume, or sometimes they spiral down the page, leaving ghost images of themselves behind. Sometimes these prints, Tara tells me, are altered by accident: a slight shift as she makes the hard crank of the press wheel, and what emerges from that plate comes as a surprise, no matter how carefully she's cut out the stencils or applied the wide swaths of ink.

There's something about them that makes you uneasy, these passenger jets and their invisible cargo: they threaten to creep out of the corner of the frame if we glance away, and then where will we be? With only that sky to seize us? A famous sculptor comes to Tara's studio, and turns to each wall, the prints hanging in their gentle rows, all those planes flying, and says, *is this about 9/11?* And his question is wary, as if to say, *because if they're all about 9/11, then I don't want to know.* So how can Tara answer?

She turns the wheel of the press and another print emerges, the blue unpredictable, volatile. *I started working on these images out of fear,* she says. It's hot in the studio, and the stenciled planes are precise, and sometimes she has to keep cutting new ones because ink stains them, they get a little bloodied, and so they're no good anymore, they'd ruin the effect. And so she has to keep cutting, hunched over on her stool, the exacto knife quite exact, exacting.

The famous sculptor says Tara must not start loving her planes too much, or else they will become too pretty, and we *don't like pretty*; no, we need that edge to make it beautiful, that little bit of *antagonie*, the pull between two opposing forces—the will to live, the lure of death—to make the image hold fast, not disintegrate the way planes are wont to do, the way any solid thing heaved up in the air will naturally incline to fall. *Okay folks,* the pilot says, so calm in the face of it, *we're beginning our final descent.*

II.

My friend Eden is afraid of flying. Whenever she boards a plane, she concentrates very hard on keeping the craft in air. *We all have to think good thoughts,* she says, shooting glances at her fellow passengers, but most of them seem oblivious, arguing with the stewardess, or with a child, or just tuning out altogether, sleeping with their heads thrown back, their mouths open in horrible wide O's, as if already struck dead. So she does it herself, thinking *the plane will fly, the plane will fly,* like an old woman at her rosary, until the stewardess comes by and taps the seats to bring them back to a full, upright position.

Tara turns the wheel again, and again. I think of her there in the dim light of the press room, and the prints accumulate, the planes leaving the hangar and taking flight—each one circumscribed by prayer, the slightest touch, but enough to keep them flying. She reminds me of her namesake, the Tibetan deity Tara. This Tara manifests in multiple, colored forms: Green Tara, for action; White Tara, of the mind; Yellow Tara, of wealth; Red Tara, for joy; and, most holy, Blue Tara for protection. Blue Tara, according to Buddhist scripture, is "the remover of obstacles." She "teaches us to transform the distorted energy of wrath and anger into the wisdom of clarity."

Tara's blue prints emerge from the roller, each one different, but each one holding steady, those planes in a holding pattern. *What I'm trying to get at,* Tara says, *is the moment just before the next thing will happen . . .* And she tells us later, her face disintegrating: *I lost my best friend in 9/11, why can't I just say it?*

Because it's unspeakable. So she rewinds time and the planes do not make their terrible turns, those cuts in the blue air. She is printing her monotypes, saying her rosary; she is dancing the Dance of Twenty-one Taras; she keeps turning the wheel, that Tibetan prayer wheel, the groaning revolutions you hear on the high ridges of the Himalayas, spinning out a continual *Om Mani Padme Huhm* into the charged air.

She hangs them with clothespins—they bend the line in a slight curve—and now I see what they remind me of so clearly: prayer flags, those fluttering cloths, edges frayed, you see strung on high ridges in Tibet. You can buy them yourself at the little hippie shop on Main, string them in your backyard to border a garden, or hang them inside to animate empty thresholds between rooms. These flags waft continuous prayers into the air—prayers for protection, prayers for peace. Sometimes it's the Wind Horse flying among the calligraphy, but most often Tara's image stamps the rough cloth again and again: duplicates of one woman guarding the skies.

III.

I have always believed in a vertical purity . . .

There's a moment in the first movement of Beethoven's violin concerto: the orchestra has been beating a careful pulse beneath the soloist's violin—a viola plucked here and there, a steady percussive beat in the background—and then suddenly, without your knowing it, the orchestra has vanished and the violin soars out there by itself, lightheaded in space. It floats untethered—no, not floating but *flailing* upward, into the stratosphere, trying to reiterate melodies the orchestra has already negotiated, but the air's too thin, it won't quite make it; the violinist tries, though, and in this striving cuts a path through the brain, stenciling its own shape: that sharp triangle of wings.

And if you listen to this music carefully—if you set aside everything else and just listen, eyes closed, hands at rest in your lap—you'll feel that violin right behind your eyes, the place where a deep pool of lamentation abides, before specific tears shape themselves for a specific grief. And just when you think the violin will have to quit, to clatter broken-stringed to the ground, a viola edges back in to help: plucking, sidling up the way you might approach someone in pain, unsure if she really wants help and so you just hold out your hands to see if she'll grab on . . .

And she does. Well, it's rather like that: the violin falls back into the orchestra's arms, and takes up the song in full force, all of them together and rejoicing at being together again, unharmed, laughing even at the way the violin got lost there for a minute. And you, the bystander: you can breathe again.

. . . and the air steps back from each body in song . . .

IV.

The prayer flags keep waving, a zephyr of praise that keeps the world's grief cooled. And I think of Galileo, his theory of falling bodies, how predictable it is now: the time it takes any two people to land. And Tara keeps printing her monotypes, untitled, the isolated planes never touching down. "The moment before the next thing . . ." Not the impact, not the explosion we've already seen—again and again—as if by watching we might somehow make amends . . .

. . . the sky a pale plate
of nothingness—nothingness—
then the cirrus-cloud tails
rushing through.

Tara delays the planes, rather like the trains of De Chirico, paralyzed by *The Enigma of the Hour*, halted, yet moving; never arriving, never departing; keeping company with the dead who don't yet know they're deceased. She is not a painter of still lifes, not an artist who would place nice figurines just so on a wrinkled cloth: statuettes of Mother Mary, perhaps, or Kuan Yin, two saints who keep their heads tilted to the side, just so, their faces ripe with compassion for those who suffer. But her monotypes are still lifes of a sort: the one plane flying still through her life. *Memento Mori*. Stalled Life. The plane stalled overhead. As if it, too, could feel a premonition and rear back, try to keep at bay whatever will happen next.

And never happens next. Not here. Not now. But grief, too, can be a secret machine that keeps humming long after you've clicked off the engine, shut the door on it, walked away. You sit in the kitchen, drinking coffee and passing the time, thinking how to decorate your rooms, those empty thresholds beckoning. Maybe you listen to Beethoven and swoop your arms through the air, a maestro conducting by proxy such music. Or perhaps you'll watch the prayer flags wave in the garden, flapping their respects to whoever passes by. But that engine keeps purring. And you might wish only for those planes to spin back into toys, harmless, seized in the hands of a child who loves them.

The italicized lines of poems throughout sections III & IV are borrowed from *The Ghost Trio*, by Linda Bierds.

Interview with Brenda Miller

1. How did you meet Tara Parsons and become interested in her work?

Tara and I met while we were both in residence at the Vermont Studio Center, an artists' residency for visual artists and writers. I had finished a writing project and decided to take advantage of being around visual artists to gain new inspiration and possible collaborations. I asked certain artists if I could simply hang around their studios and write. Tara graciously allowed me into her print-making studio, where I spent some time with her finished work and also watched her process.

2. Did you know Parsons had lost her best friend in 9/11 before she disclosed it to you in front of the sculptor? Did you talk about the issue with Parsons again? Did you have to get permission from her to reveal this secret in the essay?

I can't remember exactly when I learned her personal experience was behind the repeating images of airplanes, but the minute you saw them, especially relatively soon after 9/11 (this was in the summer of 2004), you got the sense that these planes were flying out of that moment in time. I didn't talk with her about it again, and when I told her that *Agni* was publishing the essay and wanted to use some of her images to accompany the piece, she was very happy.

3. Your meditation on Parsons' grief uses a lot of repetition, a revolving wheel, a ceaseless prayer. Was there a personal, unspeakable grief you were dealing with in writing this essay?

That's a great observation! I wouldn't say there was any particular memory or grief of my own that was playing out in the essay; I was drawing upon other images and experiences at the Vermont Studio Center, including a beautiful meditation chapel I frequented and a yoga studio that held classes several times a week. The repeating imagery of the airplanes seemed, in its own way, a kind of meditative chant or prayer, and the form of my essay must have mimicked that rhythm. When I'm on a writing retreat, especially in the presence of other writers and artists, my work becomes very intuitive and I just have to get out of the way.

4. If some truths of 9/11 are unspeakable, and if secrets are hidden truths, then have secrets taken on a new dimension after 9/11?

That's a good question, and not one for which I have an answer. When you ask this, I think about how all those people in the twin towers didn't know their lives would end or change on that morning, and how each one of them had a private story that was theirs and theirs alone. I think about how *tender* we seemed to become with one another after 9/11, as if we had all come close to that edge and realized our unspoken, and unbroken, connections.

Not Less Than 1,000 Bottles for Horseradish

Jen Hirt

MY GREAT-GRANDFATHER STARTS THE MORNING OF DECEMBER 25, 1913, WITH a gun to his head.

He wakes to a noise downstairs in his home on East 40th street in Cleveland, Ohio. His wife wakes too, but there is no rousing from their young children, among them my two-year-old grandfather. Sam Hirt investigates. He is a small Austrian, a less-than-observant Jew with very round eyes and a country of frown under a mustache so wide he looks to be all mouth, like an old baby bird with its beak shut. His forehead glows a half moon under a hairline receding at a wrecked angle. Because he and Anna were well-off, they have at the staircase a button for a downstairs light, a convenience that most homes will not have for another half decade. The light reveals a masked man who levels at him a revolver.

I won't know any of this until one hundred years later. And I hear the news not through a family story or a long-lost relative, but from the front page of a newspaper.

Two weeks before I discover the news of the robbery, my dad sends a surprising email. From the subject—Horseradish—I can half guess it's about Sam Hirt, who started our family's greenhouse business, still thriving today, by growing and selling horseradish. "Hirt's Greenhouse used to be called Hirt's Horseradish," my relatives would say when I pressed them for the few family stories they told. That single sentence was the whole "story." My imagination started and stopped with a wooden cart piled with snaggly white roots.

The message is a forward, the original sender a stranger. He's attached a photo of a small glass bottle with a crusty cork and a red and green label. *Hirt's Celebrated Horseradish*, it reads in a flourish of script descended from snake oils and hair tonics.

I've never seen one before, despite four generations of a greenhouse family, despite standing in the greenhouse Sam Hirt built, despite writing a memoir with the greenhouse at the center, despite how the bottle should have been an heirloom in a box in an attic.

I lean forward to this jpeg Rosetta Stone of clues—the peculiar full name of the business (his horseradish was *celebrated?*), and below that, "Put up by Samuel Hirt, New Sheriff Street Market, Cleveland Ohio"—the precise location of his vendor's stall. Below that, phone numbers so old they are undialable. In the attic of the Internet I quickly set myself to working through search strings involving the new clues—every variation and spelling of celebrated, horseradish, Hirt, and New Sheriff Street.

And then, there it is, the top story on the front page of the *Cleveland Plain Dealer* from December 26, 1913. The headline reads, "Wield Gun on Man, Get $739: Masked Robbers Force Citizen to March Downstairs in Night Attire."

As I read and reread, it's like Sam Hirt has gone spectral in his night attire and he's narrating this true crime drama back at me, with the intruder in control. "Turn that light out and be quick about it," the article reports the robber saying. Sam obeys with darkness. Anna calls from the bedroom. The stranger shines a handheld beam. It is a pocket lamp that, like Sam's light button, is a recent invention, and the reporter—there is no byline—will have to take a few extra sentences to explain to the readers how you can have a light in your pocket.

I notice something odd: That the shock of a *citizen* marched *downstairs in his night attire* takes precedence over a headline about open-heart surgery performed with cocaine, and news of the hemophiliac Romanov boy bruising his leg, and a feature about Rockefeller golfing in Cleveland. It seems to take precedence over Christmas and Passover and winter and the whole world. I click to the second page of the article and am shocked back in my chair by a portrait of Sam and Anna—only the second known photo of them together.

The man orders Sam to come down, and I imagine Sam must be thinking not about pocket lamps: He is thinking, What end is this? He has survived persecution in Eastern Europe, bartered his way solo onto a voyage to America, outlived one wife, worked the railroads, remarried, started his own business. And now he descends on this holiday to he knows not what.

Sam's mistake, says my brother after I email him a pdf of the article, was that he didn't have a dog. My brother's been robbed—a broken side window, his PlayStation taken. The greenhouse business that he (fourth generation Hirt) is now president of has been robbed twice, and partially as a result of that my brother owns a German shepherd. "Early warning system," he says.

Later, he texts me. "He should have used a bank. All I see in the past are mistakes I refuse to make."

My dad, meanwhile, is delighted. His favorite hobby is digging dirt on relatives dead and alive, and this dirt is golden because of its placement on the front page of the largest newspaper in the region and its narrative details. It quickly becomes the most detailed family story any of us have to tell.

The robbers, now two, direct Sam to the safe. They know exactly where it is. Cold, heavy gun to a shaking dark-haired head, and I'm sure he's shaking because he must know by now that his house has been cased and the robbers have been watching him, that he has grown complacent—perhaps a better man would sleep with a gun. What else is my great-grandfather feeling? Fury that this is how it ends, after all he's been through? Helpless in the face of six rounds loaded? Is he worried about Anna, the children? Is he cursing his mistake, whatever it was, that let these men stake out his home? He must know he can't overpower the thieves. He must know how suddenly few his options are in this time of wealth and success and all he's worked for with his horseradish business. I wonder if he wondered if he'd live.

The guy who found the bottle—I'll call him Gary—has included his contact info in his email, so my dad and brother have a meeting betwixt themselves to strategize over how to procure the bottle. If Gary wants money, they will pay no more than $250, which my dad determines is the high-end price for similar bottles on eBay.

My dad emails, calls. He makes it clear that he is "prepared to make an offer." Then he does it a second time. Silence.

I ask him what he thinks Gary is doing with the bottle. Dad thinks Gary might be contacting all the Hirts in the world and seeing who makes the best offer, and there is worry that a distant relative who has the last name but no greenhouse connection will bid high. That's how my dad operates—thinking that any person, given the chance, will take what is rightfully yours. He's so excited by the robbery article because it explains his inheritance of distrust.

A few weeks later, Gary emails to say he's going to keep the bottle for now.

Dad calls me. "It's wrong," he stammers. "Morally wrong. The Hirt family should have that bottle."

Sam clicks the combination on the second try and palms $739 in cash, which the article reports as three days of holiday profit from his horseradish stand. Today, that amount dollars up to $16,000. How long does he hold it before he hands it over? Or does he even hold it? (Of course he holds it. He counts it every day.) Does he step back and watch the robbers reach into his safe? Will Anna blame him? Does he contemplate retaliation—is there anything he can hit them with as they bend and bag his money?

Then it's over. Cloth bag cinched, pocket lamps off, thieves fleeing out the back door.

Sam calls the Third Precinct police, but they are worthless and the thieves escape. Then, and this is the only way I can make sense of the prominence of the next day's headline, he must have called the newspaper—likely the only time he spoke about the robbery.

I want the bottle.

I email Gary and ask if I can interview him on the phone about how he found it. He agrees but writes that there isn't much to say.

The story is that Gary, with a day job in information technology, had a chance to buy the rundown caretaker's house at an old Jewish cemetery in Cleveland. He'd already flipped three houses, but this one he'd keep for himself—because of "perfect neighbors." He hired "a couple of drunks" to gut the house. In the crawlspace between the top floor and the attic they found two bottles, because what else are drunks supposed to find? They showed the bottles to Gary. One was old but nondescript—Gary handed it back to the workers. The other was *Hirt's Celebrated Horseradish*. It was, he said, the first time he'd found anything interesting in an old house.

He recognized the name, because everyone in northeast Ohio seems to know our family one way or another—we've been selling plants there for over a century. The label was still bright and smooth and had not known any sun. He took two photos. That night he typed "Hirt's Celebrated Horseradish" into a search engine and the first link was the Hirt's Wikipedia page that I maintain, with the horseradish phrase that I had typed long ago when I thought the business was just "Hirt's Horseradish."

He says the bottle is in a dark cabinet, safe from the light that will ruin the label. Our conversation falls silent as we reach the part where he should offer to sell or I should offer to buy. Or he should just give it to me. Neither of us says anything. He's been difficult to talk to—I've had to rephrase and rephrase my questions to get details out of him, and more than once his tone has tripped into either impatience or annoyance. I haven't told him anything about the robbery article.

"What's your favorite thing about the bottle?" I ask, promising that it's the last question.

Gary pauses. I know he's turning that bottle in his hand, considering it. I close my eyes. I could cry. I hold my breath instead.

"It's the phrase 'Put up by'" he says. "'You just don't see that anymore. With the name. 'Put up by Samuel Hirt.'"

He's right, that's the best part of the bottle. He's a computer programmer, dealing all day with the anonymous horrors of tech language and the Internet. Five personalized words on antique glass stand out. I want to say to him, "Imagine how that would look if Samuel Hirt *happened to be your great-grandfather*," but I don't. And I think of the $3 million worth of plants and mostly plastic containers my family sells each year, none of it with anyone's full name. I think about how my dad will sell vast amounts of something ridiculous this week—like thousands of dollars of live ladybugs—but he can't get ahold of this one bottle with his grandfather's name on it. I hang up without asking for it.

The treasure map of the Internet entices me—there *must* be other Hirt's Celebrated Horseradish bottles out there. But my linguistic buzz gets subdued after a few Internet searches. Turns out that everyone in the early twentieth century deemed their horseradish celebratory because it's a bitter herb suitable for Passover Seder. With the invention of machine-made glass bottles in 1906, bottle makers designed a generic "celebrated horseradish" bottle that any up-and-coming entrepreneur could order, customized with a last name. Antique and vintage bottle websites have entire categories of "so-and-so's celebrated horseradish" bottles, like Runyan's and Lake's. The more I click through bottle sites, the less Hirt's Celebrated Horseradish seems quirky and clever and the more it seems mainstream, mass-marketed, a ready-made business. And yet, despite what seem like thousands of "celebrated horseradish" bottles catalogued online, I can't find a single Hirt's bottle. I even contact the National Bottle Museum in New York. If you ever get one, says the acquisitions guy, we'd love to add it to our collection.

We grumble sour grapes over the bottle. My brother says he's not interested in the bottle because it's a thing of the past, and the past is full of mistakes (we could have been wealthy condiment heirs, he laments, far wealthier than greenhouse heirs). My dad says what's important is the photo—that's all we really needed to see, and it gave enough info to lead to the robbery article. He decides he has other things to do and isn't going to waste his time on this. A friend advises, "You don't want that bottle. You'd have to dust it." I tell myself that Gary will take good care of the bottle—if he renovates old houses, at least he cares a little bit for the past, right?

But the truth is I want the bottle, and I can't fully explain why, and I can't fathom a reasonable dollar figure to put on it. Would it show poor judgment to call Gary and offer, say, $500? Yes. Maybe. But it seems disrespectful to offer just $50. And I want to believe there is a type of person who would just give an object like that back to the family, but I don't think that person is Gary.

At dead ends on all paths, I head back to the online newspaper archives, wondering if, in the days after the robbery, there were any follow-up articles. There were, but not about Sam. The Cleveland police acknowledged the out-of-control crime wave. There was a massive shakeup and reorganization of detectives on

December 28, 1913, a complete reassessment of how they would combat the crime that was resulting in holdups and even a shooting. Rockefeller enjoyed his holiday golfing, the Romanov heir recovered from his bruised leg (though more sinister dangers loomed for him), and the cocaine-numb heart patient died when the stitches failed. Sam, I figured, was already planning his move out of town—by 1915 he'd bought land in the countryside, in a small town called Strongsville, far from the city.

On a whim, I search for "Samuel Hirt" in the issues before the robbery, and I find that in February of 1913, he scored a day in court for refusing to pay a manufacturer for what he deemed were flawed horseradish bottles:

BOTTLES COURT ATTRACTION

Not less than 1,000 bottles of a peculiar bluish tint and used for horseradish were on exhibition in a case on trial yesterday before Common Pleas Judge Foran.

Several hundred bottles were strewn about on the floors and a couple of jurors afflicted with artificial legs had a hard time getting about.

Some of the bottles were placed on the trial table and owing to the peculiar acoustic properties of the court room the lawyers and witnesses innocently pulled off a vaudeville bell ringing stunt.

The bottles are involved in the suit for $400 instituted by the C. L. Flaccus Glass Co., Pittsburg, against Samuel Hirt, who claims in defense that many bottles were defective and unfit for bottling horseradish.

I think about the courtroom that day, what it must have looked like to see 1,000 small bottles set all over the place, 1,000 renditions of the nifty *Hirt's Celebrated Horseradish* label, like in a dream or a surrealist painting. I picture Sam Hirt's frown over those bluish bottles that will make his creamy white horseradish look rancid. I can hear the company rep asserting that they won't take them back, they're fine. I can see the reporter chuckle to himself as he puns that headline—"Bottles *Court* Attraction." I imagine the judge is annoyed with the spectacle and *someone* is about to be held in contempt, especially if anyone clinks any more bottles in the *peculiar acoustics* of the room. And let's not forget that *amputees are on the jury*, and well, *you* try to navigate that wooden floor mined with five-inch-high bottles with *your* peg leg.

There's no follow-up to the article, but I have a feeling Sam Hirt won—no one wants blue horseradish, and judging by the cash he had in his house at the end of that year, he must have been selling a normal-looking product. Besides, the Hirts tend to come out on the winning side of money. You'd have to to keep a business running for over a century.

Yet here's the serious part, the important part: Less than a year after the court case, karma caught up with miserly Sam and he lost $739 in the robbery, almost double what he was trying not to lose in court.

And here's the part that breaks my heart: There were once a thousand of his bottles all in one room, each one with that fantastic old label, and no one wanted them.

POSTSCRIPT: In November 2013, Gary walked in to Hirt's Gardens and handed my brother the bottle, for free. My dad put it in a glass case in his office, under photos of Sam Hirt. On December 23, 2013, I drove five hours to hold it in my hands for the first time.

Interview with Jen Hirt

1. Your essay combines research and speculation to not only report on but re-create the distant past. For example, when describing the robbery, you incorporate details from the 1913 newspaper article and speculate about Sam Hirt's actions and thoughts while being held at gunpoint. Can you explain the challenges of re-creating the past in a way that is factual yet engaging to the modern reader?

The past is a secret, and no one can fully clarify it for you. But creative nonfiction writers don't need the clarity of historians, who often have to cite almost every sentence to "prove" its factuality. We need the clarity of vision and voice. I guess that the technique of speculation—taking your best artistic guess as to what was likely happening—is like sharing a secret with yourself, and then translating it for a reader. The challenge is making it sound like nonfiction and not just fiction. For me, the dividing line is this: nonfiction can re-create thought and questioning; fiction, meanwhile, will invent dialogue and action. So when I use research to re-create a scene, I try to imagine less about the action and more about the interior state of mind. I rarely use direct dialogue when re-creating a scene from the past—that sounds too much like fiction to me.

2. Although your family only had a few stories, one being that "Hirt's Greenhouse used to be called Hirt's Horseradish," you "pressed" your relatives for more stories anyways. Why is such persistence important?

I think it has to do with being a Midwestern writer who left the Midwest during her formative writing years. I spent the first twenty-two years of my life in Ohio, then spent another three years in Iowa. For me, the white, upper-middle-class Midwest was a place of taciturn silence. No one ever really talked about what was really going on; on the other hand, I was a child for most of that time, not privy to adult conversation. Then, at age twenty-five or twenty-six, I found myself in Idaho, that wild inland northwest, and I was suddenly running with a cohort of writers who weren't all from the Midwest. I realized many of them had a persistent, inquisitive nature that had been nurtured in them from a younger age. I loved it. When I did become an adult, and a writer to boot, I found the courage to be more questioning of my family. However, the people who knew me from my childhood still saw me as the child whose questions could be easily dismissed. So by pressing them for more stories, I was reminding them I was an adult now; I had earned the right to hear the "real" stories. Even so, I never really got to hear any! So, when the newspaper story of the robbery popped up in an Internet search, all those years of persistent asking about stories paid off, because I knew what to do with all those details in the story, since I'd been craving them for almost two decades at that point. That's why it's important—you never know when your persistence will actually come through. So you have to keep practicing. It's like the Girl Scout motto, "Always be prepared." Here's an essayist's motto: "Always be persistent."

3. When interviewing Gary, you kept the report about the robbery of Sam Hirt a secret. When should a writer keep their hand close to their chest, and do you have any advice for crafting questions/interviewing people with suspicious motives? What are the ethical concerns?

This is a great question. When creative nonfiction writers are conducting interviews, I think that keeping their cards hidden can be a smart move. What's interesting is that I actually learned this while I was a journalist for a small town newspaper. I would often know the answer to a question I was asking of a city council member, but I would feign ignorance and ask anyway, because what I wanted was not "the answer," but "the city council member's answer," in his or her own (often inflammatory) words. So I took the same approach with Gary. I knew that in the essay I would parallel his "robbery" of the family heirloom with the robbery Sam Hirt went through. If I had told him my plan ahead of time, he would likely have become defensive—no one wants to answer to an accusation. But people do want to respond for a request for explanation. "Explain to me why . . ." is a great ace in the back pocket for essayists to haul out during interviews, even if the writer already knows exactly what's going on. Because the thing you don't know is how the person will phrase their answer. Is it ethical? The process of creating something artistic is the most ethical thing I know how to do.

Okay Forever

Barrett Swanson

I FIND THE VIDEO BURIED DEEP IN THE C: DRIVE OF MY FATHER'S COMPUTER, in a folder called "JUSTIN: LEGAL." It plays six and a half minutes from December 24, 2004, that were recorded by the front-entrance security camera at a Water Street bar in Milwaukee. The file is called "Xmas04_SWANSON_ACCIDENT," and I'll watch it hundreds of times in the coming months.

The video is at first grainy and blurred, bearing more or less the cinematographic quality of a home movie. Dark figures migrate across a cadet-blue backdrop. It's during these first ten seconds of the video that you can just barely make out two faceless figures standing toe-to-toe in the center of the frame. There's no audio. The figures mug it out while other daubs of color scuttle here and there, ghosting from one end of the bar or the other, but everything is wholly silent. The two figures could be dancing, exchanging intimacies, kissing even. But around the half-minute mark, the tracking tightens, the dimensions resolve, and the images get pulled into clarity. Here are two men, drunk, spitting taunts and admonitions through gritted teeth. Occasionally they point, at one another's face, or outside toward the sidewalk, where herds of barflies are swerving to and fro, some wearing Santa hats and ugly knit sweaters. A few people have drifted over to watch the argument, and some of the braver witnesses start pulling on each guy's elbow, offering what must be all the relevant exhortations—take it easy, let it go, have another one on me. The crowd thickens in this interval. The paradox of a crowd is that the larger the crowd grows, the harder it becomes to see the inspiration of its origin.

My brother, Justin, is the beefy guy on the right, wearing the black backward cap, a matching muscle shirt, and two earrings in each lobe. In a few hours, the ICU nurses at a nearby hospital will give my mother a Ziploc baggie containing these dented metal hoops, along with two nipple rings, a leather choker-necklace, and an argent chin stud. The camera, though twenty feet above the floor, still conveys Justin's fullback stature. He has the build of a Mason jar, stout and rounded and strong. Right now he's wearing his usual pre-punch expression of what almost looks like sadistic glee, a clown's meretricious grin. I know this expression from childhood, when he used to pummel me with gusto whenever our parents left the house. He wants the other guy to know that he's got exactly zero problem with trading blows if that's what this is going to come down to. In the video, he's acting under vague professional pretenses as a bar bouncer, a job for which he gets paid handsome cash, under the table, and one that has rather unsurprisingly supplied him with extensive knowledge about human aggression. He once told me about dragging some poor sot out of the bar by his ears after the man in question had groped a female patron, and that by the time they made it to the sidewalk, the guy's ears were starting to rip away from his skull. He once described the foul sound his carpal bones made that one time he landed a concussing punch. He has shown me how to take down a guy twice my size by slamming the butt of my palm into the assailant's thorax.

Earlier that evening, only half an hour before what takes place on the video, Justin called me from the bar, using his friend's cell phone so that I wouldn't recognize the number.

"Hello?" I answered groggily. I was home from college on winter break, lying in my childhood bedroom and staring up at the phosphorescent stars I'd once pasted onto the ceiling in haphazard constellations.

"Mr. Barrett Swanson?"

"Who is this?"

"Mr. Swanson, this is the U.S. Census Bureau. We've just been reviewing your information and wanted to know: how do you live with yourself?"

"Justin?"

"Sup, dippy?"

"Where are you?" The reception made it seem like he was traipsing through a wheat field during a windstorm. "Sounds like you're getting buffeted by some real precipitous gale-force winds there, guy."

"Are those real words or Barrett words?"

"Don't be a dick," I said.

"Come down to the bar. I'll buy you shots, find you an older woman."

"I'm in bed. We have to be at Grandma's in like ten hours."

"I know. I'm supposed to glaze the ham."

"Why is it that when you say 'glaze the ham' it sounds like a euphemism for self-abuse?"

"Because that's what I meant." In the static-glitzed background I could hear a dulcet female voice call Justin's name, telling him to hurry up. "Come on, it's Christmas. Show your brother some love."

"You're out of cigarettes, aren't you? You want me to stop at the Mobile and bring you smokes?"

"Maybe I do. Maybe I don't."

"See you tomorrow, Justin."

Around the video's one-minute mark, it looks like the other guy is attempting détente—he holds out his hand as if to shake and make up. In response, Justin grabs himself meaningfully and points. The crowd seems to swell as the other guy rears and snarls in response, his arm cocked back with intent, but his friends grab him, deactivating the attempted jab. At this point you can only see his head, there are so many people holding him back. That the Boschian tableau of my brother and the drunken patron and the anonymous watching mob is entirely silent somehow makes everything worse. In the face of the guy's theatrics, my brother stands firm, and, brazenly, stupidly, kisses his palm and waves. It's the exact same gesture my dad makes whenever angry motorists honk at him for cutting them off. It's the exact same showy semaphore I used to razz linebackers with after I split a cover-two defense and threw a corner fade for a touchdown as a high school quarterback. I understand acutely the delicious mix of peril and pluck that prompts a male from my family to behave this way, to have the gall, the temerity.

Finally, the other guy's friends corral him out the frosted-glass doors, whereupon they all migrate down the street until they disappear from view. Soon, the bar seems to heal itself. A few coworkers come over and make sure Justin is all right, and after engaging these fellas in a rather complicated-looking sequence of high-fives and fist bumps, he's left alone and the holiday's ambient good feeling seems to resume. Seconds later, a kohl-eyed brunette wearing a Santa hat and a short leather skirt swivels through the front door, and Justin turns to watch her, biting his fist, his eyes roving from ass to ankle. It's odd to see my brother like this—confident and cocksure, blustering around the bar like he knows he's being filmed.

He walks outside, where he leans against the front window and lights a cigarette. A feathery plume jets out of his mouth, rises, and disappears. A police car swooshes past, its lights going kaleidoscopically, washing the street with infant pinks and the blue of the long dead. Flurries have started to fall, and within a matter of minutes, the sidewalks look confected. Justin glances left and then right, inhales and exhales, the smoke unspooling, rising. Cars blur by. A group of bar-hoppers passes him on the sidewalk, and they look like they're singing Christmas carols.

But then it's just as Justin stomps out his cigarette and turns back to the bar's entrance that there's a visual disturbance in the right periphery of the frame, a strident streak of gray, bleary movement, and at this point, the camera's transmission glitches and loses its feed for half a second, a dark blink, but restores itself in time to see the patron who left the bar only moments ago—the other guy—a pace or two away from my brother, who himself is just now beginning to sense and register something racing toward him and now turns to look at the exact moment the guy fires his clenched fist, the impact of which lifts my brother what I swear must be two feet off the ground, so that for the briefest of instants it looks like he's levitating, and as his head arcs down toward the street before his feet follow him, he looks momentarily graceful, majestic, the snow falling in eerie slow motion behind him, but the hideous beauty of this moment ends abruptly when his skull flails back and cracks against the building's brick wall. For the remainder of the video, before the bartender finds my brother splayed out unconscious on the frozen sidewalk, before someone calls the cops, before the ambulance arrives, for these two full minutes before the video runs out and the computer's media player tells me I have the option to PLAY IT AGAIN, the man stands over my brother's body and points, taunting him.

The Glasgow Coma Scale is one of many ICU scoring systems used to determine the neurological capacities of persons who present signs of traumatic brain injury (TBI). Both EMTs and emergency room doctors are instructed to assess a cranially injured patient's eye (E), verbal (V), and motor (M) responses, which are then ranked on a scale from 1 (least responsive) to 5 (closest to normal function), meaning that, say, an E1 score would denote a patient's inability to open his eyes; a V2, that his linguistic range amounts to the screech and garble of a smart ape; and an M3, that in response to painful stimuli the patient exhibits a decorticate posture—bending his arms inward to his chest with clenched fists and locking his legs into full extension, a pose that doctors colloquially (and rather cruelly) call "the mummy baby" posture. Any total GCS score less than 9 ranks as a Severe TBI. During his ambulance ride from the snow-dusted sidewalk outside the bar to the entrance of the nearest hospital, nearly seven miles away, my brother's GCS score was very low. Upon their arrival at the ICU, my parents were whisked down to the hospital's little prayer room/chapel to meet with the chief neurosurgeon and a social worker—the hospital's way of informing the family that the patient's prognosis is dire and perhaps fatal.

I imagine Justin's emergency room arrival as a high-octane sequence from *ER*: harried but good-looking doctors in unblemished smocks jog beside his stretcher and shout abstruse medical commands. Tributaries of fresh blood trickle down his face while a female resident asks him whether he can understand what she's saying. His neck is in a foam brace, and his eyes are closed. The right side of his face is already swollen, the skin around the eye bearing the shape and elasticity of a blown bubble of gum. Even though he's unconscious, his hands fidget at his sides, his fingers bending and swooping across the air, which the nurses misinterpret as involuntary muscle spasms resulting from cerebral edema but which are actually finger spellings of ASL, a language that Justin has been studying with a kind of monastic intensity for the last few months. Later, when the nurse points out his odd digital movements, my mother will lose it. A few months ago, Justin, very eager to share his new knowledge, taught us all how to sign the ASL alphabet, and in the Intensive Care Unit, around 4:30 A.M. on Christmas Eve morning, my mother will have watched her oldest son, unconsciously, autonomically, finger-spell what she swore was the same word over and over again: "no."

We're not supposed to be here. It's Christmas Eve, and we're all supposed to be at my grandma's lake house, getting drunk on my uncle's old-fashioneds and singing woozy renditions of Bing Crosby songs. We're supposed to be unwrapping presents and *oohing* enthusiastically at the ugly sweaters we've gotten for each other. There's supposed to be eggnog and Snickerdoodles and honeyed ham. There's supposed to be a filigreed explosion of Yuletide kitsch: stuffed reindeer with googly eyes hanging from doorknobs; plastic decals of snowflakes plastered to the windows; a toy train orbiting the base of a heavily decorated tree. Someone should be asking us to remember what we did last year. But instead there is only this: my brother lying unconscious on a hospital bed, his face beaten and bloodied, a crown of gauze adorning his temple, little highways of tubes snarling up his arms.

Right now it's about 7:30 P.M. on Christmas Eve. My sister, Cat, and Mom flank Justin's bed, and they take turns soaking a rag in a bowl of ice water and scrubbing away the dried blood from his temple. Something about this scene—the silent ablutions, the stoic grief—reminds me of the *Pietà*. Cat is headlong into the sort of adolescent rebellion that will make her cringe in just a few short years but that right now finds its most obvious expression in her portmanteau wardrobe. She wears a gray (!) Mohawk, thrift-store acid-washed hip huggers, a red leather vest (whose origins are wholly unknown), and does her makeup in a way that can only be described as Ancient Egyptian, the collective effect of all of which makes her resemble Pat Benatar if Pat Benatar ever dressed up like a gay Pharaoh. She reeks of menthol cigarettes, a sick, minty miasma that both Mom and Dad ignore.

Dad sits next to me in one of the comfier chairs that the nurses brought in when they realized the rules about visiting hours weren't going to apply to our family. They have arranged the furniture around Justin's bed stadium-seating style, a feng shui that somehow invites spectation, as if the room itself were suggesting that all we can do is just sit here and watch Justin's brain decide whether he's going to live or die. His room is huge, with large city-facing windows and potted plants. Beige machines with black and green monitors draw the horizon line of his pulse. A respirator, which is connected to the oxygen mask he wears, huffs and wheezes, asthmatically.

Mom and Dad's marriage has been in a state of slow attrition these last few years, and as is often the case during these sorts of familial schisms, the pre-divorce alliances have been decided by gender. I am thus the de facto advocate of Dad's marital grievances, and Cat is Mom's, which means that she and I have been regarding one another for the last few months with the casual malice of coaches from opposing teams.

"Hungry?" Dad asks. He hasn't slept in twenty-four hours, and little psoriatic pouches have gathered under his eyes, lending him the look of a hound dog. Since before I was born, Dad has worn the same neatly trimmed Pancho Villa moustache to distract from his horseshoe hairline.

"Not really." Earlier in the day, Mom insisted Cat and I open our stockings, which she brought to the hospital. Unsure of what to do after we dutifully nibbled at our chocolate Santas, Mom urged us to open a couple of presents, to as best we could carry on with the traditions of Christmas, until someone—I can't remember who—dropped a bulky and extravagantly wrapped box on Justin's stomach, which didn't at all rouse him or make him flinch, and which reminded us of why we were there, prompting us all to agree that it would be better to hold off on presents until later, after Justin woke up.

Above me, the TV broadcasts a Christmas marathon of MTV's *The Real World*, which Cat watches absently, her chair pulled up real close to Justin's bed, her head resting on the edge of the mattress, as if she and Justin were watching the antic shenanigans of hip twentysomethings—people his age—together. Cat's position next to Justin has a *Weekend at Bernie's* falseness to it. On the other side of the bed, Mom looks raddled. Around her eyes are webs of broken capillaries, and her auburn hair has the tousled coiffure of someone who's recently awoken from a nap. She wears big square glasses and a pilled turtleneck.

"So the guy just came up and sucker-punched Justin, that's all we know?" I ask.

"He went outside to smoke a cigarette, the bartender said, and the guy ran up and punched him," Mom says. Her voice is brittle from too much crying.

"Lighting up seems like a pretty innocuous thing to do for someone to put you in the hospital."

"What are you saying?" Dad asks.

"You know how Justin can get."

"What, you think like Justin provoked him?" Cat asks.

"I'm just saying that there's probably a reason."

"Guys like that," Dad says, "don't need a reason. They go out *looking* for a fight."

"Justin wouldn't do something like that," Mom says. She looks back at Justin lying on the bed and breathing into the oxygen mask.

One thing Mom and Dad do when one of us kids has either failed to achieve something we really wanted or has fucked up in an appallingly monumental way—e.g., failing to get into our first choice for college, getting busted for underage drinking, or cheating on significant other, etc.—is that they explain the circumstances of the situation in such contortionate ways that they effectively erase your culpability in the respective failure or fuckup. Dartmouth's application requirements were excessively high; your friend's neighbors were being priggish and unreasonable when they called the cops on the party; you are a young, handsome guy and shouldn't yet tie yourself down to one girl. It's hard to ignore the fact that their airbrushing of the truth, their making you look better or less at fault than you really are, is their way of maintaining their sinless mental image of you. The frequency of these charitable excuses has increased commensurately with the worsening of their marriage, as if Mom and Dad needed to convince themselves that their festering relationship hasn't at all prevented their children from becoming model citizens. To be a good parent of suburban American children then is to be forced into a wholesale bargaining of reality, where one must continually whitewash the faults of one's progeny in order to preserve the daydream of raising the perfect child—as if mere wishing simply made it so. It occurs to me that Justin, Cat, and I are thus, perforce, supposed to serve as sterling instantiations of why it's important *to stay together for the kids.*

What I haven't admitted to anyone yet is that I'm not scared. Even though the nurses keep reminding us that even if Justin does wake up, it's all but inevitable that he will suffer from debilitating brain damage that could impair his motor skills, his speech, and his ability to comprehend reality, I remain unfazed, emotionally immobile, frozen inside. I don't know whether this is a manifestation of some sort of deep sadistic pathology lying dormant within me since birth and that I'm just now beginning to realize that I'm some kind of unfeeling sociopath who regards his brother's unconsciousness as just the next thing that has happened in his life, or perhaps it's that Justin's accident has hurtled my brain into such a state of shock that I'm unwilling to register the ghastly realities unfolding in front of me, but the truth is that I'm not worried, that I have maybe chosen to harbor the fanciful delusion that everything will eventually be OK.

One of Justin's nurses—the one who's a dead ringer for Whoopi Goldberg and who has been tending to my brother with an almost maternal sedulousness—enters the room. Even though we've only been here for fifteen hours, we have grown comfortable with these strangers intruding on our little bivouac of bereavement, carrying out their ministrations while we whisper and weep. Mom is quick to get out of the way and help out if she can, but the nurse says she just needs to quick-change Justin's gauze. A light over his head deepens his features in a way that reminds me of a Caravaggio. And just like that, with exactly no momentousness whatsoever, Justin stirs, groaning Neanderthallically, which for obvious reasons—i.e., the persistent worry that he'll surface from this horror with the intellectual capacities of a baboon—unsettles me. He opens his eyes and is swiftly resurrected into a state of total confusion, his face wounded with concern. Then he starts thrashing around the bed, convulsing and screaming. He tears the IV out of his arm. He hikes up his hospital gown and tugs the catheter off of his penis in a way that I assure you does not look painless. "Justin, Justin!" the nurse yells. Dad and I are up from our seats and stand at the edge of the bed. Mom mutters something devout. Cat covers her face with her hands and is looking through the web her fingers make, saying at intervals and with increasing volume as Justin's movements become more frantic, "Mom? Mom?" The nurse hits a button on the gadget near his bed, and within seconds, a few more nurses race into the room. They all work to restrain his arms and legs, a process which, given his considerable hulk, is not executed easily. But before they can even tighten the restraints, Justin relents and lies back, huffing raggedly. An eel of fresh blood squirms down his face.

"Justin, listen to me, honey. It's OK. You're in the ICU, you're in the hospital. Your family is here. I want to ask you a quick question, honey. You listening? I want to know if you know what today is? Do you know what day it is, Sugar? Talk to me. What day is today?"

His chest rises and falls. His mouth is twisted up, his expression rueful, almost childlike. He looks like he's on the brink of either hysterical laughter or a crying jag. His eyes pan from Cat to Mom to Dad and then to me, where they settle for a minute before they close. The silence is alive, a presence in the room. Then he opens his eyes and looks up at Mom and says, "Presents?"

Here's a memory. Justin is about twelve years old, which makes me nine, and we are watching our parents get ready for one of those rare date nights when they gussy up in their nice clothes and head out sans children and drive to their favorite Japanese restaurant where they'll split a bottle of bad wine and eat some weak suburban hibachi. Right now Mom sits on the edge of my parents' bed, looking into a compact and wiping a mar of lipstick off her front tooth, humming along to the Bette Midler playing from the bedside's tiny stereo. She wears her hair in a loose chignon and her perfume reeks of mildewed fruit. Swaddled in a hatchling-yellow blanket, a four-year-old Cat is barnacled to Mom's side. Justin and I sit on the floor and watch Dad titivate in the bedroom mirror, futzing with his moustache and the knot of his Windsor, and because he can sense us watching, he hams it up for us, doing his Rodney Dangerfield impressions, all throttle-popped eyeballs and raspy exclamations of disbelief—Hey, *I don't get no respect!* Justin and I eat this up, not because we've seen *Caddy Shack* or *Easy Money*, but because this is our father being silly, performing with Vaudevillian animation, just for us. It's one of those few times where he's cut-loose happy, giddy at the prospect of having a night alone with his wife. But even as I'm laughing, I'm growing acutely conscious of the fact that soon our ranch-style suburban home will be empty of the parental authority and the sensible code of conduct it enforces, including such provisos as NO FIGHTING, which of course means that my brother, riled from an adolescently fraught week at middle school, is going to be able to evoke and cathart his rage on the putative human punching bag little brothers everywhere are supposed to serve as. It's not like I don't understand the child-raising bromide—boys *will be boys* (a tautology that I find about as reasonable as it is poetic)—or that my brother's roughhousing *always* wandered out of the realm of sibling roughhousing and into the vaguely demarcated territory of torture, but I will say that as an inveterately sensitive young boy, in the sometimes hour-long throes of grunting struggle against my brother, I had a very tricky time parsing the differences between the expected fraternal horseplay and the diabolical violence in which my brother seemed to revel.

Sometimes my fear would be unwarranted, and we would end up watching *Big* or *The Sandlot* on the couch while our parents were out. But other times were of course different, darker. I forget how these epic brawls began. The scenes emerge out of the film fade of memory in medias res, disjointed and gauzily edged, fragmented by forgetting. And yet, during their dramatic zeniths, they do take on a high-definition clarity, a plasma-screened pixilation—that one time Justin pretzelled his legs around my stomach and squeezed with vice-like pressure until I screamed so loud I popped blood vessels in my right eye; the time he jumped off the top of the couch and landed on me, breaking my arm; the time he and his friend locked me in a closet with the light off for an hour; the time he threw me down the stairs because I wouldn't tell him what Mom had gotten him for his birthday.

Sitting here next to the hospital room's window, in the wine light of a molten sunset, what frightens me most is there were times when I was a kid that I actually prayed to my puerile idea of God—a kind of cosmic genie who would grant my every wish and cede to my every demand—and asked for something like this to happen, for Justin to get hurt so disastrously that his proclivity to beat me up would be, in turn, concussed out of him. I imagined him bloody-faced and crying. I wanted to see him hurt and puling, crawling toward me, begging for clemency. I fantasized about standing above my brother, looming, pointing. Asking him how he liked it.

It strikes none of my family members as odd that the chief neurosurgeon has decided to hold Justin's X-ray against the window, blazed to a golden foil by the erumpent morning sun, instead of just using the lightbox on the wall. It's Christmas Day, about thirty hours since Justin was wheeled into this room. The doctor has a little bejeweled Rudolph brooch clipped to his lapel. He points to the image's amorphous shapes: the dark areas indicate infarction (tissue death) or edema (abnormal accumulation of fluid), and the bright, diaphanous portions signify calcification, hemorrhaging, or the displacement of bone. There's a hideous gorgeousness to the pictures. Seven contusions bleed across my brother's brain in dark blotches that are somehow reminiscent of those black scourges of communism and fascism that overtook world maps in those old duck-and-cover films. Mom asks about our options. The doctor says that depends on a number of factors, but right now we need to let his brain heal on its own, as best it can. He tells us with professional alacrity to sit tight and keep praying. There's an odd apparitional quality to the shapes that have developed on the celluloid sheet that the doc still holds pressed against the windowpane, as if what were being displayed here were not so much an index of damage done to my brother's brain, but an imprint of his ghost, a scanner-blast of his soul.

Here's the truly distressing double bind about hospital gift shops: usually you purchase a gift because you want to surprise the giftee with something heartfelt and special, an emblem of true affection, but because the medical events that bring someone to the hospital typically occur without warning, you thus have no time to dash out and select something useful or thoughtful or etc., all of which is problematic because, of course, any sentient convalescent is going to know the various merchandise that a standard gift shop carries and will thusly be able to surmise that you picked out the sea-salt chocolates and the "Get Well" Mylar balloon and the Calvin and Hobbes sympathy card you gave them *at the hospital gift shop*, meaning that the whole act of giving the gift is going to look obligatory, carried out in deference to trite social conventions and just so that you could say you brought the person something, which maybe isn't that big of a deal if the person is just a friend or a colleague or some distant relative you never much see, but when the person is your brother and his chances of survival are touch and go and his cognitive abilities at this point are on par with a drowsy infant's, the paucity of gift choices can run you down to the point where you're sobbing in public with your face pressed against the stuffed pectoral of an oversized Foghorn Leghorn, which of course draws concerned looks from the other gift shop patrons until eventually the kind lady behind the register races over and offers you a diet soda and crackers, allowing you to sit on a stool in the shop's back office where a little black-and- white TV is playing the Packers game, which makes you feel better for a little while, even if we're down 21–17 at half.

No one who knew Justin well would have thought that at twenty-three years old he'd end up bouncing at a Water Street bar. In high school, he cultivated an image of himself as a brooding *artiste*, a sensitive type who eschewed any and all displays of machismo.[1] Aside from being an indispensable part of the high school's award-winning choir, Justin was also in a professional performing group that did shows at events and festivals all across Wisconsin and to which he contributed a winning stage presence and a syrupy baritone.[2] Along with his thespian achievements, Justin was also a prodigiously gifted painter, influenced by the controlled technique of Celan, the creative caprice of early Jackson Pollock, and the theoretical pursuits of Jim Dine. As a high school senior, Justin had shows at privately owned galleries and even sold some of his work. His was a talent

---

1. When I told him that I had tried out and made the varsity football team, as a quarterback, his response was to look at me and blink very slowly before walking away.
2. Full disclosure: I, too, was a member of this group in my more impressionable early teenaged years, when the group's uniform of jazz shoes, pink cummerbunds, black tuxedo shirts, and chartreuse silk vests didn't seem like that big of a threat to one's reputation as a tough-guy jock.

so refined that he was accepted to the Minneapolis College of Art and Design (MCAD)—one of the best art schools in the country—on a full scholarship. And the truth was that Justin couldn't wait to leave our hometown. Growing up in an affluent suburb of Milwaukee, which was known for its big shopping plaza, was for him variously like walking around the soundstage of *Leave It to Beaver* and the set of *Blue Velvet*. The houses were huge and new and set back on green, fragrant yards that were vigilantly groomed by hired help. Around town, in grocery stores, denizens regarded one another with a kind of caffeinated cheeriness that I can now only describe as a model for customer service. For Justin, a flannel-wearing, teenaged misanthrope who rode skateboards and smoked Camels and sometimes drank Vodka out of Evian bottles before school, this was a suffocating environment, one that he started rebelling against by the time he hit puberty. But at MCAD he thrived socially and excelled academically. By the end of his second semester, his work was so roundly admired by his peers and the faculty that one of the printmaking professors asked him to be his TA for the following fall semester, an unprecedented achievement for a freshman, according to the school's lore.

But then one night, in one of life's weird, unforeseen peripeteias, Justin went to his studio, threw on the newest Spiritualized album, and apparently got so intoxicated that the world contracted to something bitter and small, a reality trivial enough to abandon. At some point that night, he destroyed most of his paintings, kicking holes into canvases, using his hands to shred sketchpads. Then he went to a party in Uptown, by Lake Calhoun, and no one's exactly sure what happened after that. He surfaced the next morning, at around 7:30 A.M., while walking down a residential road in St. Paul, nearly seventeen miles away from where he lived, and as he watched joggers huffing down the sidewalk and a delivery man toss newspapers out of a slow-moving car and a sprinkler spray a helix of dawn-glinted water onto a nearby front lawn, he looked down at his bleeding hands and his torn shirt and realized that he needed to come home.

Mom drove up to Minneapolis and moved him out of his dingy little apartment, and they drove the six hours back home. Ruined and then annealed by his misfortunes at MCAD, he lived in the carpeted room of our home's flood-damaged basement, got a job as a sales associate at Restoration Hardware, and started hanging out with some of his old friends, whose puny ambitions didn't take them very far from home. He got a tattoo and pierced his lip. I rarely saw him during the period, but when I did, we would occasionally engage in drunken, bumbling tête-à-têtes. Whenever I brought up those fights from childhood, he would misremember the episodes or contend they weren't as bad as I had characterized them. "Besides," he said, "that I beat you up probably made you more sensitive, which is why you're such a good writer. So, really, you can thank me for that." He'd usually punctuate these aperçus by tipping the top of his beer bottle toward me, as if we were coming to some sort of agreement.

When he saved up enough money, he moved out. Having worked in restaurants while going to school in Minneapolis, he was quickly hired as a sous-chef at a posh trattoria on the East Side, in the Third Ward, and soon fell into the cash-burning rhythms of the late-night service industry, which is to say that whenever he wasn't working, Justin was eating at friends' restaurants, out partying at the local bars, or inviting his service-industry friends over for dawn-seeing parties. The owner of the bar, whom Justin met during this period of heavy carousing, asked Justin to do some part-time bouncing work, under the table, to which he ultimately agreed.[3]

On the night of the assault, before he showed up at the bar, Justin had been dancing in the half-time show at the Milwaukee Bucks game. The incongruity of these events startles me—one minute he's doing a round-off at the Bradley Center wearing spandex and jazz shoes, and the next, he's grabbing his unit and telling a bar patron to go fuck himself. It turned out that one of his old friends from the performing group had become a Bucks' cheerleader and asked Justin to dance with her because that night's choreography featured a lot of complicated lifts and gymnastic maneuvers, which a guy of Justin's strength and stature could execute effortlessly. After the show, as he and the rest of the male dancers drank celebratory beers with the cheerleaders, toasting one another on a job well done, Justin got a call from his boss at the bar—an oleaginous guy who every time I saw him wore tortoiseshell glasses and a Boston Red Sox cap—asking that he come in to help with the Christmas Eve crowd. An hour or so later, Justin showed up and was informed about a patron who had been making lewd advances toward the female bartender all night. Justin tapped the guy on the shoulder and the two

---

3. Justin's failure to sign a contract was something I later regarded as breathtakingly stupid, especially since it allowed the bar owner to wangle his way out of paying Justin's worker's compensation, thus causing all sorts of financial/legal migraines for my parents. When Justin finally left the hospital, the boss had the gall to visit our house and bring Justin an X-Box 360 as a gesture of apology and recompense. What a guy.

had a conversation near the entrance, the mute surveillance camera version of which I watched hundreds of times a few months later. I never found out what exactly was said between them—whether my brother stepped outside of his duties as bouncer and provoked the guy. In fact, it seemed any possible culpability on Justin's part was rinsed away by the fact that he ended up unconscious in the hospital.

At night, there's an odd, oneiric quality to the ICU. All the overhead fluorescents are turned off, but the galaxy of power indicators on everyone's machines are of course still on, so that when you walk down the hallway and peek into other people's rooms it looks like each person is recumbently manning the switchboard of a space station. All the nurses shuffle here and there in their sensible sneakers, whispering to one another updates about this or that. I drift back to Justin's room with an intoxicated listlessness, my body still humming with the memory of the cigarette I stole from Cat's purse and sucked down in the underground parking lot only minutes ago. Inside the room, everyone's asleep. Mom lies on the cot next to the window, using her pea coat as a blanket. Cat is crumpled up like a crustacean in the chair, her hands clasped together prayer-like and wedged between her knees, her Mohawk mashed against her pillow. Dad lies collapsed on the floor like he fell through the roof, using a rolled-up jacket as bedding. Justin is awake. His right eye is still swollen to a slit, the bruise around it the color of a wine stain, its shape no more symmetrical than a Rorschach blot. But his left eye is trained on me in the sort of way children under two will stare dazedly at you when you make little gaga faces at them. He looks like he's trying to figure out who I am, but he doesn't seem alarmed or concerned about my presence in the room. I walk over to him and hold his hand, acutely aware that I'm reenacting just about every hospital scene from every TV drama, major motion picture, and novel that I have consumed in my heavily mediated nineteen years. I resist the urge to say something genre-appropriate like *we're gonna get through this.* He looks down at our embrace, indifferent, just curious. The machine beside him aspirates and contracts. I can feel my father's snoring in my chest, even from across the room.

"How are you doing, guy?" I whisper. "Do you know who I am?" The nurses have encouraged us to ask him this question, to get him to tell us our names. Even though it feels ridiculous—it's the type of thing you quiz your friends' children on: *Hey, who's that, can you say Barr-ett?*—the nurses say it's important we test his memory with easy ones, as if our identities were simply a matter of trivia. I keep meaning to ask the nurses what we should say on the off-chance that Justin can't answer this question. What are we supposed to ask him then?

"Justin, it's your brother," I say, right up close to his ear. "Do you know my name?"

The machine behind him beeps as it draws a green cliffside of his pulse. He closes his eyes, inhales and exhales steadily, a sound I've grown to covet.

For an entire day, the guy who did this to my brother ran free. He went home that night, slept, and woke up on Christmas morning. Throughout the first day in the hospital, I spent what turned out to be an unhealthy amount of time imagining what sorts of Yuletide fun was being had by my brother's assailant. Maybe he wore something festive, a red cable-knit sweater and green chinos. Maybe he styled his hair with pomade. Maybe he visited his grandmother in the nursing home. Maybe he and his father reconciled after years of strained communication. Maybe he ladled out chili at a soup kitchen, or washed bed sheets at a homeless shelter. Maybe he sang Christmas carols at the VFW. Maybe he drank more. Maybe he masturbated. Maybe he played football in a snowy park with a group of rowdy friends. Maybe he and his girlfriend had gentle sex next to a dawn-facing window. Maybe he was a good person. Maybe he wasn't normally like this. Maybe he was just blotto and made a bad decision. Maybe he went to church and was washed with little geodes of light beaming through the stained glass. Maybe he prayed that my brother was OK.

But it turned out that on Christmas night, my brother's assailant was at a family party, eating shrimp cocktail and standing with some of his male relatives in front of a big-screened TV. At a certain point, after all the small talk (and what I imagine had to have been more than a judicious amount of brandy-laden eggnog), the guy began cheerfully alluding to knocking someone out at Water Street bar. In one of the incident's weirder twists of fate, my uncle, who's something of a socialite and has a long roster of friends and just so happened to be at this party, overheard the assailant's bluster. My uncle excused himself from his conversation, walked over to the scrum of men by the TV, and asked the assailant whether this incident had occurred at Justin's bar. The guy nodded, smiling. My uncle then gave him a rather merciful ultimatum: either the guy turn himself in or he would do the honors and call the cops. When he related the story to us an hour or so later, he said that never once in his life had he felt more like Columbo.

It's only when I'm urged to get out of the ICU for the night and told to go see some friends, and thus leave these hallways fumigated with grief and disease, and finally exit the hospital's automatic sliding doors that open along their tracks with a respiratory hiss, that I am overwhelmed by an incredible soaring relief. I'm nineteen and on winter break from my second year at college and, though my brother is in the hospital, I'm still able to go out into the December evening and find a friend's party and drink watery beer and meet a pert twentysomething with a body as lean and lissome and uninjured as mine and we can find a spare bedroom in which to have grunting, acrobatic sex. This is my plan. Driving my mother's Ford Blazer, I'm smoking a Camel, blasting some insipid hip-hop hit by someone named Nelly, and careening down the I-94 expressway, roaring out of the city and headed for the suburbs. It's only after I call my friend Sam, and learn that another friend's parents are out of town and that she's having a kegger, and drive over to her house and enter without knocking and am swarmed by friends and strangers alike who, I shit you not, form a little line to greet me with their sympathy and concern that I begin to understand the unbelievable advantages of having a moribund brother in the hospital. *Barrett, take a quick pull of this scotch I got here. Have a ciggy with me, Swany? Give me an update about yer bro's prognostication, guy. Yo, b-man, what's the story with your bruh? Your brother's in the hospital, that must be horrible, huh? Do you want to play beer pong with me?* After someone intubates me with a beer bong and after I do a keg-stand, I'm feeling better, shined-up and mercurial, able to converse prolixly with everyone, and I explain the dire state of Justin's condition with an anesthetized fluidity. I realize that I'm the god of this story, that I can make it seem as bad as I want, that I am in control of my brother's life in this moment. I consider telling them about the contusions and the posttraumatic seizures and the one pamphlet I read about dealing with a brain-damaged loved one, but as the scotch marinates my bloodstream, my summary of his prognosis takes a markedly optimistic turn and instead I tell everyone he's nearly back to normal and the doctors say he'll be out of the hospital in just a few days. As long as I can convince them of this story, as long as people think Justin's going to be OK, then at least for the night, he will be.

Spend a week in the ICU and roam the hospital's scrubbed and sanitized hallways and you'll eventually notice the squadron of janitors and cleaning people who wear khaki jumpsuits and assiduously wax and sterilize just about every linoleum surface until all the hallways are lemon-scented and gleaming, lest the perfume of blood and carrion waft into other rooms and remind the ill and infirm of their ultimate fate. As much as the doctors and nurses and staff work to facilitate convalescence, there seems to be a tandem and equivalent effort to expurgate death from the hospital's interior-decorative flavor. Looked at closely, a hospital—with its white walls and white-coated doctors and white-smocked nurses and white bed sheets and white towels and white glinting floors and white Formica surfaces—appears to be one large contrivance toward the heavens, a huge portal through which the diseased and dying can pass seamlessly into the white light.

Sleep-deprived and commensurately bereft, I begin to resent the hospital for this curatorial effort, because the truth is that at a certain point in this line of thinking, you begin to associate the monochromatic environment with the very thing its sterility and cleanliness and homey ambiance are trying desperately to conceal—namely, your own mortality—which makes the whole thing a lot like listening to a car salesman tell you he's offering a real sweet deal while you test-drive a Buick without brakes. Exacerbating my anger about all this is the fact that nearly every doctor, RN, CNA, resident, and intern looks hale and happy and gorgeous, their skin untouched by any blemish or mole or liver spot, their bodies gym-fit and libidinous.

Cosmetic discrepancies between staff and patients notwithstanding, the true root of my outsized anger stems from the fact that my brother can't remember my name. Every night, when everyone else is asleep, I return to his bedside and ask him to tell me who I am. Invariably, he just stares and stares. At times his confusion is so total that it looks contrived and I almost think he's putting me on. I have to restrain myself from smacking his head and shouting *come on, do it, asshole, say my fucking name!* It occurs to me that what would be way worse than Justin dying would be Justin living and having no memory. Because if he surfaces from this neurological oblivion with no recall of who I am or what we've been through together, then in a certain way it'll be me who has died as a result of that punch. He won't associate my face with the person who came to every single one of his gallery openings, the person who used to beg him to perform that skateboarding trick one more time in the driveway, the person who despite everything always looked up to him with the brightest of eyes. Maybe it's selfish, but the truth is that during these moments I begin to grieve the loss of the person who lived inside my brother's head—the person I was to him.

By the 30th of December, almost everyone has stopped by—family, friends, coworkers, his boss. When his ex-girlfriend stops by and massages his feet, Justin wakes up and smiles at her knowingly, as if the sensation were an inside joke between them. And yet he doesn't respond when she calls him by his pet name, "Mister." Everyone brings him an offering, but given his prognosis—i.e., a traumatic brain injury—it's hard not to see most of their gifts as cruel: board games, crossword puzzles, the new Lincoln biography. When one of his friends hands me a 1,000-piece jigsaw puzzle (which I know that motherfucking asshole bought in the gift shop; I saw it), I say, expressing my nineteen-year-old-little-brother indignation, "Dude, seriously?" For the most part, though, I labor hard to hide my contempt for their thoughtlessness, to return their words of concern with appreciative hugs. Everyone brings flowers. Whole nomenclatures of tulips and daffodils and water lilies line the windowsill and tables. The room blazes with these little bonfires of color to which Justin, when he's awake and trying to stay engaged, will point and say things like, "What's with that dog?" Or "Gimme that firework there." Most of the time he just sleeps.

And yet he has made substantial progress. The doctors keep our expectations in check by reminding us that just because Justin can recognize Mom and Dad and knows what day it is, it doesn't mean that his will be a full recovery. They warn of aphasia, posttraumatic seizures, ataxia, depression, and memory loss. We try to exercise cautious optimism, but it's difficult not to be heartened by his improvements. Yesterday, our aunt, fresh in from Las Vegas where she lives, stopped by to check on Justin. A few months ago, Nancy paid for Justin's veneers—all his life his teeth had huge gaps between them, going all the way back to his molars, which somehow made him look feral and Flintstonean. When she came over to Justin's bed and said, "Hiya, sweetheart, how you feeling?" Justin looked over at her and opened his cheeks really wide—it was a smile without emotion, like a monkey's—to reveal a mouth full of teeth so straight and pristine they could have sold toothpaste. Nancy screamed with laughter and Mom started to cry, both of them realizing that this meant Justin not only knew who Nancy was but could remember something from a few months ago, which suggested that his long-term memory was in working order.

But the true bellwether of his progress occurred earlier this morning when Justin was scheduled for a shower. The youngest of his nurses—a fist-bitingly pretty CNA who goes to UWM and who laughed at my joke about Justin's boss looking like a sober Robert Downey Jr.—approached Justin's bed, brandishing a little scrub tub and loofa. "Looks like I'm the one who's washing you today." I squeezed Justin's arm until he looked at me with a kind of resigned weariness— the way everyone looks when they're in line at the DMV—and I mouthed, *You lucky bastard*. No response. "Do you understand me, Justin? I'm gonna help you take a shower today." He looked at the girl and then looked at me, clearly confused, as if she were reciting Arabic poetry. "Justin?" A silence followed, a brief interlude of beeping machines and voices coming from another room. I could already see the joke hanging in his eyes. Without any facial expression or vocal affectation whatsoever, Justin said, "I think you should meet my mom first."

My tuxedo shirt is too tight and Justin's pant legs are too long. He's fixing his cufflinks while I tend to his crooked boutonnière. It's late August, years later, and it's his wedding day. We're standing under an amber sky in the little rhomboid of grass outside his house on the east side of Milwaukee, waiting for one of Justin's other groomsmen to arrive before we head over to Astor Hotel, where Justin will swap vows with his fiancée. (Justin will buy Cat and me tequila shots at the cash bar, and Mom and Dad will be amicable for the night, despite their recent divorce). Birds chitter overhead and the wind is like something out of Tarkovsky, strong and tidal-sounding, a portent of obscure meaning. The yard's trees and shrubbery are so green they look like they've been treated with food coloring. He keeps his hair Agassi-short, and his stocky stature fills out his tux rather sharply. His face and neck are lightly shellacked with sweat.

"Nervous?" I ask.

He frowns and then feints a jab at my face, and I flinch, and for half a second I think he's serious, but he breaks into a smile, so I lasso my arms around his neck and bring him in for a hug.

"Big day," he says, smiling. "Huge day."

The straggler arrives and we all get into our cars. Justin and I ride together, in his crummy, grumbling car, and soon we're speeding down Kinnickinnic Avenue, past the hipster thrift stores and fair-trade cafés and organic pet depots, and we cross the bridge into the Third Ward, with its boutiques and its spas and its aura of opulence. We're on Water Street when we hit a red light. Broken glass speckles the cement and coruscates in the sun. Crushed beer cans pock the sidewalk. A discarded stiletto is stuck in a nearby sewer grate. The street has an eerie evacuated quality, as if God made a mistake and only the frat boys and party girls got raptured.

There's not one scar on his face. The last vestige of the assault was the scar tissue that mottled his temple like cottage cheese, but it disintegrated about a year ago. That's not to say that his recovery was without hitches. His was an Iliad of cognitive rehabilitation. After getting discharged from the hospital, Justin spent nearly two months on the couch, slack-jawed and sedentary, and watched staggering amounts of syndicated TV. *Star Trek* and *Seinfeld* were among his favorites. At times his confusion was precocious—adorable even. When someone called the house for Justin and I'd hand him the phone, he would stare at the device for upwards of thirty seconds, seemingly perplexed about what he was supposed to do with this odd gadget. I had to show him how to hold it against his ear. Other times, he'd walk into a room, forget why he was there, and utter non sequiturs like "Well, how do I fashion *this* news report?" In the middle of the night, he took to sneaking into Cat's bedroom, and without expression, throwing his balled-up socks at her sleeping face, trying to be funny, but actually sort of freaking Cat out. But there were moments where he'd look at you with a kind of abused confusion and then say something cryptic like "You don't look like you." He went to physical therapy and cognitive therapy and slept on the couch. In spits and spells, he had memory lapses, the most disturbing of which involved him forgetting that he had been beaten up and then trying to leave the house. Because of his neurological fragility we were forbidden from letting Justin go out on his own, lest any slight bump or chance bop of the head trigger a hemorrhaging afterclap. One time he got so insistent about leaving that he pushed Dad, who was blocking the front door, to the ground. Still, after nearly six months, he recovered. As the civil and criminal trials were being adjudicated, if at a glacial pace, my brother decided to drop the criminal charges against his assailant. When I asked him about this act of strange mercy, he said, "At that point in my life, that could have been me on the other end of that punch."

The red light is long, but we don't mind. The wedding can't start without the groom and his best man. Justin has put on *Purple*, the Stone Temple Pilots' album, which is one of those records that's so thematically perfect that you never have to skip to the next song, since each one has a kind of anthemic quality, as if Scott Wieland were eulogizing every hue and nuance of your sad, disastrous adolescence, and with the windows down, wearing tuxedos, my brother and I are singing full-throatedly and well, *Leeeeeee-vin' on a souuuuuthern train, on-ly yesterday—*

The light turns green, but Justin has his eyes closed as he belts the song's chorus. He's drumming the wheel and swaying his head back and forth, and I laugh as cars start honking behind us. It could be his buzz cut or his late-summer sienna tan, but Justin's face retains a youthfulness so stark that he looks younger than I do. And maybe it's the occasion and his pre-wedding jitters, but for a minute I feel like the older brother and am momentarily overcome with the urge to tell him a story, to assure him that he's ready for this, that he need not worry about what comes next, that no matter what, I'll be right here and everything will be OK forever and ever. Things that during the crisis of childhood I wish he would have said to me. The truth is, of course, that the story does not end here, at the stoplight beneath the cerulean wash of a Wisconsin sky, does not end as I close my eyes and join Justin in this moment of willed blindness. Nor does it end in this darkness, as I listen, among the blare of music and beeping cars, for the sound of my brother's voice. And though this is not the ending of our story, it's the one I keep telling myself, the one I think that in the wake of all that has happened my brother and I just might be willing to believe.

Interview with Barrett Swanson

1. Have any secret feelings you kept hidden in your subconscious been revealed to you since writing this essay?

This question makes me think of the old E. M. Forster quote "How do I know what I think till I see what I say?" It took me roughly ten years to summon the courage to write about this event—publishing stuff about my family isn't a natural inclination—so there weren't too many emotional stones left unturned before I sat at my desk. Perhaps some fugitive emotions were chased down during the course of composition—more than anything, my anger (relentless and omnidirectional) surprised me—but I'd say that rather than revealing new emotions, the essay allowed me to live with the ones I was already aware of, to organize the mess of lived experience into a cogent story. A quote from Delillo seems more suitable then: "Writing is a concentrated form of thinking."

2. The essay has a precise analysis about how parents handle their children's failures: "To be a good parent of suburban American children then is to be forced into a wholesale bargaining of reality, where one must continually whitewash the faults of one's progeny." Is whitewashing a form of telling a half-truth? What advice do you have for nonfiction writers who see a whitewashed situation—especially within a family—and want to call it out for what it is?

Sheesh. Reading that sentence again makes me wince a little, especially since it sounds like I'm castigating suburban parents, which wasn't entirely my intention. Part of the trouble stems from the diction, since "whitewash" implies awareness, and in most cases, I don't think we are consciously aware of the extent to which we are telling ourselves a generous fib about ourselves or our loved ones. Allow me to use this space to amend that statement. By my lights, the most intense interpersonal relationships—being a parent, sibling, or spouse—necessarily involve a kind of shared delusion, because when you commit yourself to someone, or share a roof with them, you are in some sense agreeing to see the world from their eyes. As a member of a family, this shared delusion is radically intensified, if for no other reason than you grow up among the same set of people, all of whom have their own unique fears and ambitions, which doubtlessly inflect the shared history you all create together. It bends and crimps the shape of your own perceptions, too. Unsurprisingly, that history—those stories that we tell each other—consists of partial truths, half-facts, muddled gospels. Make no mistake: sometimes those stories are pernicious and require urgent revision. Other times, though, we might recognize that those half-truths were simply the stories we needed to tell ourselves in order to weather bleak and troubling times. Properly understood, those stories might strike us as generous and necessary, balms for fresh burns. Though I'm loath to offer blanket prescriptions, I suppose my advice for nonfiction writers who want to shine light on a whitewashed situation within a family would be to avoid the easy interpretation, the strident denunciation. Hunt for complexity. Aim to clarify rather than condemn. Who knows. Perhaps such a procedure will help you locate a broad and proper mercy.

3. When essayists write about a trauma, they rarely have a surveillance tape of the exact moment to watch hundreds of times. Could you have written this essay without that tape?

The surveillance tape was the railing I clung to when descending into the first draft. While I was trying to make heads or tails of how best to characterize the emotional contours of my brother's extended hospitalization, the scuffle at the bar was comparably easier to write because I could simply report what I had seen on the tape. Still, this story had been needling me for years, so I'm sure it would have made its way onto the page even if I didn't have that file.

4. What is your relationship with your brother like now?

My brother and I are very close. Few people share with me such an extensive catalog of memories and cultural references, and so whenever we see each other after a long spell apart, a manic intensity infuses our interactions, a preening one-upmanship, where within minutes of picking me up from the airport, he'll be doing Al Pacino impressions, quoting zingers from *Adventures in Babysitting* (a celluloid favorite from our youth), ribbing me about my unkempt beard, bragging about the status of his bank account. And suddenly, even though I'm a thirty-year-old man with a retreating hairline, a decent job, and a lettered disposition, I somehow become my brother's little brother again, deferential and admiring, always trying to win his approval, ever angling to make him laugh. It is a role I return to effortlessly, with deep gratitude, if for no other reason than I know just how close we all were to losing him.

Three Takes on a Jump

Jill Christman

Take One

I am five. We live on an island off the coast of Massachusetts and I want to jump off the roof of our one-story house and into the sand. My mother's boyfriend, a deep-sea fisherman by the name of Captain Bill with red hair and a boat named after my mother, says no, I may not jump off the roof. From here, the golden sand looks deceptively soft. Like a pillow. Almost springy. I am five and I want to jump.

This is a favorite story from the maritime era of our family history—right up there with the half-roasted turkey flying from the oven on Captain Bill's boat and sliding around the pitching galley like a greased pig, and the lobsters knotted onto the Christmas tree by a nautical Santa. (I claim the lobsters were alive—shimmying crustaceans! salty elves!—but everybody else says boiled. Were they red? I cannot remember. I remember their wiggling claws shaking the branches.)

Like the turkey and the lobsters, the house-jumping story has been told and retold until everybody is sure of the details, the way it all went down. Today, I am not so sure. Sitting around a picnic table thirty years after the fact, I mention to my partially assembled family that there's a thing called "shareability"—the reason we all know the details of the jumping story is because we've been refining the script for years, sharing the story. The story we think we know has more to do with the telling, and retelling, than it does with memory. In other words, ours is a corroborative tale produced with all the witnesses in the same room—except, in this case, I realize I was the only one who was there, the only actual witness, and the story I'm hearing might not be the one I remember. *It's called shareability*, I say. For this piece of psychological trivia, I am eyed skeptically over the lips of beer bottles.

Everybody knows the person who makes up stories in *this* family and it's sure not them.

I'm the hero in the shared version, so I should just let it rest, let it fly, but in my line of work, these things matter, and all I'm saying is we need to look into the gaps here. For example, what am I doing on the roof in the first place? What fool let a five-year-old climb a ladder, scale the warm, black shingles, peer down into the sand, and consider jumping? How did I get there? I am five!

But let the picnic table family finish the story. On the roof I am, and I am *insisting* on jumping down. There is a standoff. Finally, the sea captain boyfriend says, *Go ahead*. This is everybody's favorite part, and everybody but me chimes in like a Greek chorus (after all, as the subject of the story, the little girl with all the chutzpah, somehow my participation would be unseemly). *Go ahead*, he said. He never thought she'd actually do it, never, but Jill didn't hesitate. She marched, she *marched*, right to the edge of the roof and jumped off. She landed like a sack of potatoes—*a sack of potatoes!*—in the sand and then, and then, she stood right up, brushed off her pants, and said, "There."

There!

There.

Take Two

Okay, so this is the roof-jumping story I remember and I'm foolish to do so, because in this version I spin myself as a victim instead of a hero, a girl who is desperate instead of tough. In memory, I am older than five. Seven or maybe even eight. Same house, same roof, same sand. My brother and his pack of boys feature here. Let's say there are four of them all together, all older than me, all utterly antagonistic. There are no adults in this story. The boys have climbed on the roof and pulled the ladder up. I want them to slide the ladder down so I can climb up, too. They refuse. They're taunting me. I'm the girl, the baby, the worthless, whiny one. Then, my brother lowers the ladder down to me. *All right, he says, come on up.* Oh joy! I am part of the pack! I am nearly a boy! I scamper up and hurry to the peak of the roof. I can see the ocean from here!

The boys scuttle down the ladder like cockroaches down the side of a refrigerator, flipping the ladder down into the sand as the last one reaches solid ground. It was a trick. I am stuck. Hours pass. Soon, darkness will fall. The boys come and go, but now the talk turns to sand monsters and other creatures of the beach night. I no longer want to be up. I want to be down. I beg, I plead. They laugh. This is such a good one.

At some point, the boys toss up a garbage bag: large, black, Hefty. They want to know whether the bag will work as a parachute. The bag is my only way down. I cannot remember how long I wait. Finally, I shake out the bag, holding the edges rolled tight in both fists. I am hopeful the air will come in to break my fall.

This story has a moral: A garbage bag does *not* work as a parachute. Don't try it.

There is no "there!" here. I land, I hurt, I cry. I tell on the creeps when my mother gets home.

Take Three

No third version exists, although this same black roof has featured in decades of failed dreams in which my featherless arms move in futile wingbeats and I cannot fly (do I lack confidence?). But there is the thing I *know* to be true: I *did* jump off that roof and into the sand. My body remembers what it feels like to hit.

Sand is not as soft as it looks. Sand, when arrived at from a height of at least ten feet—Hefty bag or no—receives its guest with only slightly more benevolence than concrete. Sand is ground rock, after all. When I hit, the air left my lungs like a balloon clapped between two bricks. I felt the blow, the sharp emptying of my lungs, and then their refusal to fill again. Chest down, lifting my face from the sand, grit in my eyes, my nose, stuck to my lips, I could not breathe. No matter whose version is true, I hadn't expected this. I was sure the sand would be soft, or at least softer. I was a child.

Interview with Jill Christman

1. Essayists tend to come to creative nonfiction through circuitous routes. Will you share with us how you became interested in the genre?

At the University of Oregon in the early nineties, I wanted more than anything to be a writer, but I was too afraid. My dream of traveling by Jeep with my handsome, rakish, zoom-lens-toting photographer boyfriend (problem #1: there was no such person) and writing the kind of feature-length articles on grieving elephants and matriarchal hyenas that would ignite imaginations, open wallets, and quite possibly save the whole planet (problem #2: the editors at *National Geographic* seemed to have lost my phone number) had fizzled like a marshmallow held too close to the fire in my first course on pyramid structure. By the time I'd made it through grammar for reporters, my journalistic aspirations had dropped, flaming, into the embers. I abandoned the journalism program and wandered over into the English building; at least, I figured, I'd get to *read.*

So after I graduated with a degree in English literature and women's studies, instead of taking the leap into an MFA program, I heeded the advice of Lorrie Moore's narrator in the classic story "How to Become a Writer": *First, try to be something, anything, else.* Spoiler: my future lay in the writing and teaching of memoir and essays, but the twenty-two-year-old me didn't know that as she scanned the want ads—in the newspaper!—for some kind, *any* kind, of employment that required a college degree. One ad caught my eye and my fancy: research assistant and coordinator of the Dynamics Lab in the Department of Psychology at my alma mater.

2. The concept of "shareability" is fascinating in light of creative nonfiction's struggle with secrets, family stories, and half-truths. However, not many writers know about it. How did you learn about it, and what is it, exactly?

My boss at the Dynamics Lab in the Department of Psychology, who has become a life-long friend and mentor, was a dynamo—a genius, really—and when I joined her lab, her research into memory, specifically memory for traumatic events, was deepening. She had developed a theory called "shareability":

Shareability theory (Freyd 1983, 1990, 1993) proposes that internal (e.g., perceptual, emotional, imagistic) information often is qualitatively different from external (e.g., spoken, written) information, and that such internal information is often not particularly shareable. The theory further proposes that the communication process has predictable and systematic effects on the nature of the information representation such that sharing information over time causes knowledge to be reorganized into more consciously available, categorical, and discrete forms of representation, which are more shareable.[1]

3. So the composition of "Three Takes on a Jump" has clearly been influenced by your understanding of "shareability." Will you give us another example?

Even if you and I were in the same park, seeing and hearing the same excited chickadee on the same checkered picnic blanket with shared tuna sandwiches under a single cottonwood tree with the wind picking up as recently as an hour ago, our memories of that span of time will be different because we have brought to that moment our different brains, different fears, different distractions, desires, backgrounds, aesthetics—and on and on. Our stories will diverge—unless, as the theory of shareability tells us, we make the internal *external* by talking about our afternoon picnic, sharing the story of the bee that landed on Henry's nose, how his big eyes crossed in horror, how he stayed stock-still until his mother (that's me) flicked it off and his sister ran screaming. Ah, yes, we all remember the day we were having the picnic and the bee landed on Henry's nose! We will talk about it with Grammy when we see her, shoring up the details, remembering—together—the version we discussed, the details of the perky chickadee and the stinky tuna and the blowing cottonwood leaves falling away to be replaced by a clean, shared narrative of Henry's wide-eyed, frozen fear. Unless—and this is where "Three Takes on a Jump" comes in—*unless* we do something to interrogate and disrupt that shared memory as I did the day with my family when I said, "Wait. No. This is *not* the story I remember. I didn't *want* to jump off that roof!"

---

1. Https://scholarsbank.uoregon.edu/xmlui/bitstream/handle/1794/62/defineshareability.html?sequence=1.

4. What advice do you have for essayists and especially memoirists who are struggling with how to tell their family story that diverges from what the rest of the family claims is the story?

I once heard writer Cheryl Strayed, of *Wild* fame, talking about what she called the "emotional revelatory trajectory" and advising the assembled student memoirists to "write the truth, the truer, and the *truest*."

"How true is true enough?" I challenge my students. "How do you know when I've arrived at my *truest* story? You can't fact-check my heart. You can't check references on my deepest desire." In the end, only I know for sure my deepest emotional truth—*My body remembers what it feels like to hit*—but I believe it's my responsibility to land on the thing that is the *truest*. No matter how many jumps it takes.

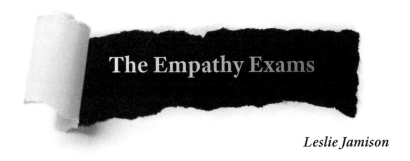

The Empathy Exams

Leslie Jamison

MY JOB TITLE IS MEDICAL ACTOR, WHICH MEANS I PLAY SICK. I GET PAID BY the hour. Medical students guess my maladies. I'm called a Standardized Patient, which means I act toward the norms of my disorders. I'm standardized-lingo SP for short. I'm fluent in the symptoms of preeclampsia and asthma and appendicitis. I play a mom whose baby has blue lips.

Medical acting works like this: you get a script and a paper gown. You get $13.50 an hour. Our scripts are ten to twelve pages long. They outline what's wrong with us—not just what hurts but how to express it. They tell us how much to give away, and when. We are supposed to unfurl the answers according to specific protocol. The scripts dig deep into our fictive lives: the ages of our children and the diseases of our parents, the names of our husbands' real-estate and graphic-design firms, the amount of weight we've lost in the past year, the amount of alcohol we drink each week.

My specialty case is Stephanie Phillips, a twenty-three-year-old who suffers from something called conversion disorder. She is grieving the death of her brother, and her grief has sublimated into seizures. Her disorder is news to me. I didn't know you could seizure from sadness. She's not supposed to know either. She's not supposed to think the seizures have anything to do with what she's lost.

Stephanie Phillips

Psychiatry

SP Training Materials

CASE SUMMARY: You are a 23-year-old female patient experiencing seizures with no identifiable neurological origin. You can't remember your seizures but are told you froth at the mouth and yell obscenities. You can usually feel a seizure coming before it arrives. The seizures began two years ago, shortly after your older brother drowned in the river just south of the Bennington Avenue Bridge. He was swimming drunk after a football tailgate. You and he worked at the same miniature golf course. These days you don't work at all. These days you don't do much. You're afraid of having a seizure in public. No doctor has been able to help you. Your brother's name was Will.

MEDICATION HISTORY: You are not taking any medications. You've never taken antidepressants. You've never thought you needed them.

MEDICAL HISTORY: Your health has never caused you any trouble. You've never had anything worse than a broken arm. Will was there when it was broken. He was the one who called for the paramedics and kept you calm until they came.

Our simulated exams take place in three suites of purpose-built rooms. Each room is fitted with an examination table and a surveillance camera. We test second- and third-year medical students in topical rotations: Pediatrics, Surgery, Psychiatry. On any given day of exams, each student must go through "encounters"—their technical title—with three or four actors playing different cases.

A student might have to palpate a woman's ten-on-a-scale-of-ten pain in her lower abdomen, then sit across from a delusional young lawyer and tell him that when he feels a writhing mass of worms in his small intestine, the feeling is probably coming from somewhere else. Then this med student might arrive in my room, stay straight-faced and tell me that I might go into premature labor to deliver the pillow strapped to my belly, or nod solemnly as I express concern about my ailing plastic baby: "He's just so quiet."

Once the fifteen-minute encounter has finished, the medical student leaves the room and I fill out an evaluation of his/her performance. The first part is a checklist: Which crucial pieces of information did he/she manage to elicit? Which ones did he/she leave uncovered? The second part of the evaluation covers affect. Checklist Item 31 is generally acknowledged as the most important category: "Voiced empathy for my situation/problem." We are instructed about the importance of this first word, *voiced.* It's not enough for someone to have a sympathetic manner or use a caring tone of voice. The students have to say the right words to get credit for compassion.

We SPs are given our own suite for preparation and decompression. We gather in clusters: old men in crinkling blue robes, MFA graduates in boots too cool for our paper gowns, local teenagers in ponchos and sweatpants. We help each other strap pillows around our waists. We hand off infant dolls. Little pneumatic baby Doug, swaddled in a cheap cotton blanket, is passed from girl to girl like a relay baton. Our ranks are full of community-theater actors and undergrad drama majors seeking stages, high-school kids earning booze money, retired folks with spare time. I am a writer, which is to say: I'm trying not to be broke.

We play a demographic menagerie: young jocks with ACL injuries, and business executives nursing coke habits. STD Grandma has just cheated on her husband for the first time in forty years and has a case of gonorrhea to show for it. She hides behind her shame like a veil, and her med student is supposed to part the curtain. If he's asking the right questions, she'll have a simulated crying breakdown halfway through the encounter.

Blackout Buddy gets makeup: a gash on his chin, a black eye, and bruises smudged in green eye shadow along his cheekbone. He's been in a minor car crash he can't remember. Before the encounter, the actor splashes booze on his body like cologne. He's supposed to let the particulars of his alcoholism glimmer through, very "unplanned," bits of a secret he's done his best to keep guarded.

Our scripts are studded with moments of flourish: Pregnant Lila's husband is a yacht captain sailing overseas in Croatia. Appendicitis Angela has a dead guitarist uncle whose tour bus was hit by a tornado. Many of our extended family members have died violent Midwestern deaths: mauled in tractor or grain-elevator accidents, hit by drunk drivers on the way home from Hy-Vee grocery stores, felled by a Big Ten tailgate—or, like my brother Will, by the aftermath of its debauchery.

Between encounters, we are given water, fruit, granola bars, and an endless supply of mints. We aren't supposed to exhaust the students with our bad breath and growling stomachs, the side effects of our actual bodies.

Some med students get nervous during our encounters. It's like an awkward date, except half of them are wearing platinum wedding bands. I want to tell them I'm more than just an unmarried woman faking seizures for pocket money. *I do things!* I want to tell them. *I'm probably going to write about this in a book someday!* We make small talk about the rural Iowa farm town I'm supposed to be from. We each understand the other is inventing this small talk and we agree to respond to each other's inventions as genuine exposures of personality. We're holding the fiction between us like a jump rope.

One time a student forgets we are pretending and starts asking detailed questions about my fake hometown—which it happens, if he's being honest, is his *real* hometown—and his questions lie beyond the purview of my script, beyond what I can answer, because in truth I don't know much about the person I'm supposed to be or the place I'm supposed to be from. He's forgotten our contract. I bullshit harder, more heartily. *That park in Muscatine!* I say, slapping my knee like a grandpa. *I used to sled there as a kid.*

Other students are all business. They rattle through the clinical checklist for depression like a list of things they need to get at the grocery store: *sleep disturbances, changes in appetite, decreased concentration.* Some of them get irritated when I obey my script and refuse to make eye contact. I'm supposed to stay swaddled and numb. These irritated students take my averted eyes as a challenge. They never stop seeking my gaze. Wrestling me into eye contact is the way they maintain power—forcing me to acknowledge their requisite display of care.

I grow accustomed to comments that feel aggressive in their formulaic insistence: *that must really be hard* [to have a dying baby], *that must really be hard* [to be afraid you'll have another seizure in the middle of the grocery store], *that must really be hard* [to carry in your uterus the bacterial evidence of cheating on your husband]. Why not say, *I couldn't even imagine*?

Other students seem to understand that empathy is always perched precariously between gift and invasion. They won't even press the stethoscope to my skin without asking if it's okay. They need permission. They don't want to presume. Their stuttering unwittingly honors my privacy: *Can I . . . could I . . . would you mind if I—listened to your heart?* No, I tell them. I don't mind. Not minding is my job. Their humility is a kind of compassion in its own right. Humility means they ask questions, and questions mean they get answers, and answers mean they get points on the checklist: a point for finding out my mother takes Wellbutrin, a point for getting me to admit I've spent the last two years cutting myself, a point for finding out my father died in a grain elevator when I was two—for realizing that a root system of loss stretches radial and rhyzomatic under the entire territory of my life.

In this sense, empathy isn't just measured by Checklist Item 31—*voiced empathy for my situation/problem*—but by every item that gauges how thoroughly my experience has been imagined. Empathy isn't just remembering to say, *that must be hard*—it's figuring out how to bring difficulty into the light so it can be seen at all. Empathy isn't just listening, it's asking the questions whose answers need to be listened to. Empathy requires inquiry as much as imagination. Empathy requires knowing you know nothing. Empathy means acknowledging a horizon of context that extends perpetually beyond what you can see: an old woman's gonorrhea is connected to her guilt is connected to her marriage is connected to her children is connected to the days when she was a child. All this is connected to her domestically stifled mother, in turn, and to her parents' unbroken marriage; maybe everything traces its roots to her very first period, how it shamed and thrilled her.

Empathy means realizing no trauma has discrete edges. Trauma bleeds. Out of wounds and across boundaries. Sadness becomes a seizure. Empathy demands another kind of porousness in response. My Stephanie script is twelve pages long. I think mainly about what it doesn't say.

Empathy comes from the Greek *empatheia*—*em* (into) and *pathos* (feeling)—a penetration, a kind of travel. It suggests you enter another person's pain as you'd enter another country, through immigration and customs, border-crossing by way of query: *What grows where you are? What are the laws? What animals graze there?*

I've thought about Stephanie Phillips's seizures in terms of possession and privacy—that converting her sadness away from direct articulation is a way to keep it hers. Her refusal to make eye contact, her unwillingness to explicate her inner life, the very fact that she becomes unconscious during her own expressions of grief, and doesn't remember them afterward—all of these might be a way to keep her loss protected and pristine, unviolated by the sympathy of others.

"What do you call out during seizures?" one student asks.

"I don't know," I say, and want to add, *but I mean all of it.*

I know that saying this would be against the rules. I'm playing a girl who keeps her sadness so subterranean she can't even see it herself. I can't give it away so easily.

Leslie Jamison

Ob-Gyn

SP Training Materials

CASE SUMMARY: You are a 25-year-old female seeking termination of your pregnancy. You have never been pregnant before. You are five-and-a-half weeks but have not experienced any bloating or cramping. You have experienced some fluctuations in mood but have been unable to determine whether these are due to being pregnant or knowing you are pregnant. You are not visibly upset about your pregnancy. Invisibly, you are not sure.

MEDICATION HISTORY: You are not taking any medications. This is why you got pregnant.

MEDICAL HISTORY: You've had several surgeries in the past but you don't mention them to your doctor because they don't seem relevant. You are about to have another surgery to correct your tachycardia, the excessive and irregular beating of your heart. Your mother has made you promise to mention this upcoming surgery in your termination consultation, even though you don't feel like discussing it. She wants the doctor to know about your heart condition in case it affects the way he ends your pregnancy, or the way he keeps you sedated while he does it.

I could tell you I got an abortion one February or heart surgery that March—as if they were separate cases, unrelated scripts—but neither one of these accounts would be complete without the other. A single month knitted them together; each one a morning I woke up on an empty stomach and slid into a paper gown. One depended on a tiny vacuum, the other on a catheter that would ablate the tissue of my heart. *Ablate?* I asked the doctors. They explained that meant burning.

One procedure made me bleed and the other was nearly bloodless; one was my choice and the other wasn't; both made me feel—at once—the incredible frailty and capacity of my own body; both came in a bleak winter; both left me prostrate under the hands of men, and dependent on the care of a man I was just beginning to love.

Dave and I first kissed in a Maryland basement at three in the morning on our way to Newport News to canvass for Obama in 2008. We canvassed for an organizing union called Unite Here. *Unite Here!* Years later, that poster hung above our bed. That first fall we walked along Connecticut beaches strewn with broken clam shells. We held hands against salt winds. We went to a hotel for the weekend and put so much bubble bath in our tub that the bubbles ran all over the floor. We took pictures of that. We took pictures of everything. We walked across Williamsburg in the rain to see a concert. We were writers in love. My boss used to imagine us curling up at night and taking inventories of each other's hearts. "How did it make you feel to see that injured pigeon in the street today?," etc. And it's true: we once talked about seeing two crippled bunnies trying to mate on a patchy lawn—how sad it was, and moving.

We'd been in love about two months when I got pregnant. I saw the cross on the stick and called Dave and we wandered college quads in the bitter cold and talked about what we were going to do. I thought of the little fetus bundled inside my jacket with me and wondered—honestly *wondered*—if I felt attached to it yet. I wasn't sure. I remember not knowing what to say. I remember wanting a drink. I remember wanting Dave to be inside the choice with me but also feeling possessive of what was happening. I needed him to understand he would never live this choice like I was going to live it. This was the double blade of how I felt about anything that hurt: I wanted someone else to feel it with me, and also I wanted it entirely for myself.

We scheduled the abortion for a Friday and I found myself facing a week of ordinary days until it happened. I realized I was supposed to keep doing ordinary things. One afternoon, I holed up in the library and read a pregnancy memoir. The author described a pulsing fist of fear and loneliness inside her—a fist she'd carried her whole life, had numbed with drinking and sex—and explained how her pregnancy had replaced this fist with the tiny bud of her fetus, a moving life.

I sent Dave a text. I wanted to tell him about the fist of fear, the baby heart, how sad it felt to read about a woman changed by pregnancy when I knew I wouldn't be changed by mine—or at least, not like she'd been. I didn't hear anything back for hours. This bothered me. I felt guilt that I didn't feel more about the abortion; I felt pissed off at Dave for being elsewhere, for choosing not to do the tiniest thing when I was going to do the rest of it.

I felt the weight of expectation on every moment—the sense that the end of this pregnancy was something I *should* feel sad about, the lurking fear that I never felt sad about what I was supposed to feel sad about, the knowledge that I'd gone through several funerals dry-eyed, the hunch that I had a parched interior life activated only by the need for constant affirmation, nothing more. I wanted

Dave to guess what I needed at precisely the same time I needed it. I wanted him to imagine how much small signals of his presence might mean.

That night we roasted vegetables and ate them at my kitchen table. Weeks before, I'd covered that table with citrus fruits and fed our friends pills made from berries that made everything sweet: grapefruit tasted like candy, beer like chocolate, Shiraz like Manischewitz—everything, actually, tasted a little like Manischewitz. Which is to say: that kitchen held the ghosts of countless days that felt easier than the one we were living now. We drank wine and I think—I know—I drank a lot. It sickened me to think I was doing something harmful to the fetus because that meant thinking of the fetus as harmable, which made it feel more alive, which made me feel more selfish, woozy with cheap Cabernet and spoiling for a fight.

Feeling Dave's distance that day had made me realize how much I needed to feel he was as close to this pregnancy as I was—an impossible asymptote. But I thought he could at least bridge the gap between our days and bodies with a text. I told him so. Actually I probably sulked, waited for him to ask, and then told him so. *Guessing your feelings is like charming a cobra with a stethoscope*, a boyfriend told me once. Meaning what? Meaning a couple of things, I think—that pain turned me venomous, that diagnosing me required a specialized kind of enchantment, that I flaunted feelings and withheld their origins at once.

Sitting with Dave, in my attic living room, my cobra hood was spread. "I felt lonely today," I told him. "I wanted to hear from you."

I'd be lying if I wrote that I remember what he said. I don't. Which is the sad half-life of arguments—we usually remember our side better. I think he told me he'd been thinking of me all day, and couldn't I trust that? Why did I need proof?

Voiced concern for my situation/problem. Why did I need proof? I just did.

He said to me, "I think you're making this up."

This meaning what? My anger? My anger at him? Memory fumbles.

I didn't know what I felt, I told him. Couldn't he just trust that I felt something, and that I'd wanted something from him? I needed his empathy not just to comprehend the emotions I was describing, but to help me discover which emotions were actually there.

We were under a skylight under a moon. It was February beyond the glass. It was almost Valentine's Day. I was curled into a cheap futon with crumbs in its creases, a piece of furniture that made me feel like I was still in college. This abortion was something adult. I didn't feel like an adult inside of it.

I heard *making this up* as an accusation that I was inventing emotions I didn't have, but I think he was suggesting I'd mistranslated emotions that were already there—attaching long-standing feelings of need and insecurity to the particular event of this abortion; exaggerating what I felt in order to manipulate him into feeling bad. This accusation hurt not because it was entirely wrong but because it was partially right, and because it was leveled with such coldness. He was speaking something truthful about me in order to defend himself, not to make me feel better.

But there was truth behind it. He understood my pain as something actual and constructed at once. He got that it was necessarily both—that my feelings were also made of the way I spoke them. When he told me I was making things up, he didn't mean I wasn't feeling anything. He meant that feeling something was never simply a state of submission, but always, also, a process of construction. I see all this, looking back.

I also see that he could have been gentler with me. We could have been gentler with each other.

We went to Planned Parenthood on a freezing morning. We rummaged through a bin of free kids' books while I waited for my name to get called. Who knows why these children's books were there? Meant for kids waiting during their mothers' appointments, maybe. But it felt like perversity that Friday morning, during the weekly time slot for abortions. We found a book called *Alexander*, about a boy who confesses all his misdeeds to his father by blaming them on an imaginary red-and-green striped horse. *Alexander was a pretty bad horse today.* Whatever we can't hold, we hang onto a hook that will hold it. The book belonged to a guy named Michael from Branford. I wondered why Michael had come to Planned Parenthood, and why he'd left that book behind.

There are things I'd like to tell the version of myself who sat in the Planned Parenthood counseling room, the woman who studiously practiced cheerful unconcern. I would tell her she is going through something large and she shouldn't be afraid to confess its size, shouldn't be afraid she's "making too big a deal of it." She shouldn't be afraid of not feeling enough, because the feelings will keep coming—different ones—for years. I would tell her that commonality doesn't inoculate against hurt. The fact of all those women in the waiting room, doing the same thing I was doing, didn't make it any easier.

I would tell myself: maybe your prior surgeries don't matter here, but maybe they do. Your broken jaw and your broken nose don't have anything to do with your pregnancy except they were both times you got broken into. Getting each one fixed meant getting broken into again. Getting your heart fixed will be another burglary, nothing taken except everything that gets burned away. Maybe every time you get into a paper gown you summon the ghosts of all the other times you got into a paper gown; maybe every time you slip down into that anesthetized dark it's the same dark you slipped into before. Maybe it's been waiting for you the whole time.

Stephanie Phillips

Psychiatry

SP Training Materials (Cont.)

OPENING LINE: "I'm having these seizures and no one knows why."

PHYSICAL PRESENTATION AND TONE: You are wearing jeans and a sweatshirt, preferably stained or rumpled. You aren't someone who puts much effort into your personal appearance. At some point during the encounter, you might mention that you don't bother dressing nicely anymore because you rarely leave the house. It is essential that you avoid eye contact and keep your voice free of emotion during the encounter.

One of the hardest parts of playing Stephanie Phillips is nailing her affect—*la belle indifference*, a manner defined as the "air of unconcern displayed by some patients toward their physical symptoms." It is a common sign of conversion disorder, a front of indifference hiding "physical symptoms [that] may relieve anxiety and result in secondary gains in the form of sympathy and attention given by others." *La belle indifference*—outsourcing emotional content to physical expression—is a way of inviting empathy without asking for it. In this way, encounters with Stephanie present a sort of empathy limit case: the clinician must excavate a sadness the patient hasn't identified, must imagine deeply into a pain Stephanie can't fully experience herself.

For other cases, we are supposed to wear our anguish more openly—like a terrible, seething garment. My first time playing Appendicitis Angela, I'm told I manage "just the right amount of pain." I'm moaning in a fetal position and apparently doing it right. The doctors know how to respond. *I am sorry to hear that you are experiencing an excruciating pain in your abdomen,* one says. *It must be uncomfortable.*

Part of me has always craved a pain so visible—so irrefutable and physically inescapable—that everyone would have to notice. But my sadness about the abortion was never a convulsion. There was never a scene. No frothing at the mouth. I was almost relieved, three days after the procedure, when I started to hurt. It was worst at night, the cramping. But at least I knew what I felt. I wouldn't have to figure out how to explain. Like Stephanie, who didn't talk about her grief because her seizures were already pronouncing it—slantwise, in a private language, but still—granting it substance and choreography.

Stephanie Phillips
Psychiatry
SP Training Materials (Cont.)

ENCOUNTER DYNAMICS: You don't reveal personal details until prompted. You say you wouldn't call yourself happy. You say you wouldn't call yourself unhappy. You get sad some nights about your brother. You don't say so. You don't say you have a turtle who might outlive you, and a pair of green sneakers from your gig at the mini-golf course. You don't say you have a lot of memories of stacking putters. You say you have another brother, if asked, but you don't say he's not Will, because that's obvious—even if the truth of it still strikes you sometimes, hard. You are not sure these things matter. They are just facts. They are facts like the fact of dried spittle on your cheeks when you wake up on the couch and can't remember telling your mother to fuck herself. *Fuck you* is also what your arm says when it jerks so hard it might break into pieces. *Fuck you fuck you fuck you* until your jaw locks and nothing comes.

You live in a world underneath the words you are saying in this clean white room, *it's okay I'm okay I feel sad I guess.* You are blind in this other world. It's dark. Your seizures are how you move through it—thrashing and fumbling—feeling for what its walls are made of.

Your body wasn't anything special until it rebelled. Maybe you thought your thighs were fat or else you didn't, yet; maybe you had best friends who whispered secrets to you during sleepovers; maybe you had lots of boyfriends or else you were still waiting for the first one; maybe you liked unicorns when you were young or maybe you preferred regular horses. I imagine you in every possible direction, and then I cover my tracks and imagine you all over again. Sometimes I can't stand how much of you I don't know.

I hadn't planned to get heart surgery right after an abortion. I hadn't planned to get heart surgery at all. It came as a surprise that there was anything wrong. My pulse had been showing up high at the doctor's office. I was given a Holter Monitor—a small plastic box to wear around my neck for twenty-four hours, attached by sensors to my chest—that showed the doctors my heart wasn't beating right. The doctors diagnosed me with SVT—supraventricular tachycardia—and said they thought there was an extra electrical node sending out extra signals—*beat, beat, beat*—when it wasn't supposed to.

They explained how to fix it: they'd make two slits in my skin, above my hips, and thread catheter wires all the way up to my heart. They would ablate bits of tissue until they managed to get rid of my tiny rogue beatbox.

My primary cardiologist was a small woman who moved quickly through the offices and hallways of her world. Let's call her Dr. M. She spoke in a curt voice, always. The problem was never that her curtness meant anything—never that I took it personally—but rather that it meant nothing, that it wasn't personal at all.

My mother insisted I call Dr. M to tell her I was having an abortion. What if there was something I needed to tell the doctors before they performed it? That was the reasoning. I put off the call until I couldn't put it off any longer. The thought of telling a near-stranger that I was having an abortion—over the phone, without being asked—seemed mortifying. It was like I'd be peeling off the bandage on a wound she hadn't asked to see.

When I finally got her on the phone, she sounded harried and impatient. I told her quickly. Her voice was cold: "And what do you want to know from me?"

I went blank. I hadn't known I'd wanted her to say, *I'm sorry to hear that,* until she didn't say it. But I had. I'd wanted her to say something. I started crying. I felt like a child. I felt like an idiot. Why was I crying now, when I hadn't cried before—not when I found out, not when I told Dave, not when I made the appointment or went to it?

"Well?" she asked.

I finally remembered my question: did the abortion doctor need to know anything about my tachycardia?

"No," she said. "Is that it?" Her voice was so incredibly blunt. I could only hear one thing in it: *Why are you making a fuss?* That was it. I felt simultaneously like I didn't feel enough and like I was making a big deal out of nothing—that maybe I was making a big deal out of nothing *because* I didn't feel enough, that my tears with Dr. M were runoff from the other parts of the abortion I wasn't crying about. I had an insecurity that didn't know how to express itself—that could attach itself to tears or else their absence. *Alexander was a pretty bad horse today.* When of course the horse wasn't the problem. Dr. M became a villain because my story didn't have one. It was the kind of pain that comes without a perpetrator. Everything was happening because of my body or because of a choice I'd made. I needed something from the world I didn't know how to ask for. I needed people—Dave, a doctor, anyone—to deliver my feelings back to me in a form that was legible. Which is a superlative kind of empathy to seek, or to supply: an empathy that rearticulates more clearly what it's shown.

A month later, Dr. M bent over the operating table and apologized. "I'm sorry for my tone on the phone," she said. "I didn't understand what you were asking." It was an apology whose logic I didn't entirely understand. It had been prompted. At some point my mother had called her to discuss my upcoming procedure—and had mentioned how upset I'd been by our phone conversation.

Now I was lying on my back in a hospital gown. I was woozy from the early stages of my anesthesia. I felt like crying all over again, at the memory of how powerless I'd been on the phone—powerless because I needed so much from her, a stranger—and how powerless I was now, lying flat on my back and waiting for a team of doctors to burn away the tissue of my heart. I wanted to tell her I didn't accept her apology. I wanted to tell her she didn't have the right to apologize—not here, not while I was lying naked under a paper gown, not when I was about to get cut open again. I wanted to deny her the right to feel better because she'd said she was sorry.

Mainly, I wanted the anesthesia to carry me away from everything I felt and everything my body was about to feel. In a moment, it did.

I always fight the impulse to ask the med students for pills during our encounters. It seems natural. Wouldn't baby Doug's mom want an Ativan? Wouldn't

Appendicitis Amy want some Vicodin, or whatever they give you for a 10 on the pain scale? Wouldn't Stephanie Phillips be a little more excited about a new diet of Valium? I keep thinking I'll communicate my pain most effectively by expressing my desire for the things that might dissolve it. Which is to say, if I were Stephanie Phillips, I'd be excited about my Ativan. But I'm not. And being an SP isn't about projection; it's about inhabitance. I can't go off-script. These encounters aren't about dissolving pain, anyway, but rather seeing it more clearly. The healing part is always a hypothetical horizon we never reach.

During my winter of ministrations, I found myself constantly in the hands of doctors. It began with that first nameless man who gave me an abortion the same morning he gave twenty other women their abortions. *Gave.* It's a funny word we use, as if it were a present. Once the procedure was done, I was wheeled into a dim room where a man with a long white beard gave me a cup of orange juice. He was like a kid's drawing of God. I remember resenting how he wouldn't give me any pain pills until I'd eaten a handful of crackers, but he was kind. His resistance was a kind of care. I felt that. He was looking out for me.

Dr. G was the doctor who performed my heart operation. He controlled the catheters from a remote computer. It looked like a spaceship flight cabin. He had a nimble voice and lanky arms and bushy white hair. I liked him. He was a straight talker. He came into the hospital room the day after my operation and explained why the procedure hadn't worked: they'd burned and burned, but they hadn't burned the right patch. They'd even cut through my arterial wall to keep looking. But then they'd stopped. Ablating more tissue risked dismantling my circuitry entirely.

Dr. G said I could get the procedure again. I could authorize them to ablate more aggressively. The risk was that I'd come out of surgery with a pacemaker. He was very calm when he said this. He pointed at my chest: "On someone thin," he said, "you'd be able to see the outlines of the box quite clearly."

I pictured waking up from general anesthesia to find a metal box above my ribs. I remember being struck by how the doctor had anticipated a question about the pacemaker I hadn't yet discovered in myself: How easily would I be able to forget it was there? I remember feeling grateful for the calmness in his voice and not offended by it. It didn't register as callousness. Why? Maybe it was just because he was a man. I didn't need him to be my mother—even for a day—I only needed him to know what he was doing. But I think it was something more.

Instead of identifying with my panic—inhabiting my horror at the prospect of a pacemaker—he was helping me understand that even this, the barnacle of a false heart, would be okay. His calmness didn't make me feel abandoned; it made me feel secure. It offered assurance rather than empathy, or maybe assurance was evidence of empathy, insofar as he understood that assurance, not identification, was what I needed most.

Empathy is a kind of care, but it's not the only kind of care, and it's not always enough. I want to think that's what Dr. G was thinking. I needed to look at him and see the opposite of my fear, not its echo.

Every time I met with Dr. M, she began our encounters with a few perfunctory questions about my life—*What are you working on these days?*—and when she left the room to let me dress, I could hear her voice speaking into a tape recorder in the hallway: *Patient is a graduate student in English at Yale. Patient is writing a dissertation on addiction. Patient spent two years living in Iowa. Patient is working on a collection of essays.* And then, without fail, at the next appointment, fresh from listening to her old tape, she bulleted a few questions: *How were those two years in Iowa? How's that collection of essays?*

It was a strange intimacy, almost embarrassing, to feel the mechanics of her method so palpable between us: *engage the patient, record the details, repeat.* I was sketched into Cliffs Notes. I hated seeing the puppet strings; they felt unseemly—and without kindness in her voice, the mechanics meant nothing. They pretended we knew each other rather than acknowledging that we didn't. It's a tension intrinsic to the surgeon-patient relationship: it's more invasive than anything, but not intimate at all.

Now I can imagine another kind of tape—a more naked, stuttering tape; a tape that keeps correcting itself, that messes up its dance steps:

Patient is here for ~~an abortion~~ for ~~a surgery to burn the bad parts of her heart~~ for a medication to fix her heart because the surgery failed. Patient is staying in the hospital for ~~one night~~ ~~three nights~~ five nights until we get this medication right. Patient ~~wonders if people can bring her booze in the hospital~~ likes to eat graham crackers from the nurse's station. Patient cannot be released until she runs on a treadmill and her heart prints a clean rhythm. Patient recently got an abortion but we don't understand why she wanted us to know that. Patient didn't ~~think she~~ hurt at first but then she did. Patient ~~failed to use protection and~~ failed to provide an adequate account of why she didn't use protection. ~~Patient had a lot of feelings. Partner of patient had the feeling she was making up a lot of feelings.~~ Partner of patient is supportive. Partner of patient is spotted in patient's hospital bed, repeatedly. Partner of patient is caught kissing patient. Partner of patient is charming.

Patient is ~~angry disappointed~~ angry her procedure failed. Patient does not want to be on medication. Patient wants to know if she can drink alcohol on this medication. She wants to know how much. She wants to know ~~if two bottles of wine a night is too many~~ if she can get away with a couple of glasses. Patient does not want to get another procedure if it means risking a pacemaker. Patient wants everyone to understand that this surgery ~~is~~ isn't a big deal; wants everyone to understand she is stupid for crying when everyone else on the ward is sicker than she is; wants everyone to understand her abortion is ~~also about~~ definitely not about the children her ex-boyfriends have had since she broke up with them. Patient wants everyone to understand ~~it wasn't a choice~~ it would have been easier if it hadn't been a choice. Patient understands it was her choice to drink while she was pregnant. She understands it was her choice to go to a bar with a little plastic box hanging from her neck, and get so drunk she messed up her heart graph. Patient is patients, plural, which is to say she is multiple—mostly grateful but sometimes surly, sometimes full of self-pity. Patient ~~already understands~~ is trying hard to understand she needs to listen up if she wants to hear how everyone is caring for her.

Three men waited for me in the hospital during my surgery: my brother and my father and Dave. They sat in the lounge making awkward conversation, and then in the cafeteria making awkward conversation, and then—I'm not sure where they sat, actually, or in what order, because I wasn't there. But I do know that while they were sitting in the cafeteria a doctor came to find them and told them that the surgeons were going to tear through part of my arterial wall—these were the words they used, Dave said, *tear through*—and try burning some patches of tissue on the other side. At this point, Dave told me later, he went to the hospital chapel and prayed I wouldn't die. He prayed in the nook made by the propped-open door because he didn't want to be seen.

It wasn't likely I would die. He didn't know that then. Prayer isn't about likelihood anyway, it's about desire—loving someone enough to get on your knees and ask for her to be saved. When he cried in that chapel, it wasn't empathy—it was something else. His kneeling wasn't a way to feel my pain but to request that it end.

I learned to rate Dave on how well he empathized with me. I was constantly poised above an invisible Checklist Item 31. I wanted him to hurt whenever I hurt, to feel as much as I felt. But it's exhausting to keep tabs on how much someone is feeling for you. It can make you forget that they feel too.

I used to believe that hurting would make you more alive to the hurting of others. I used to believe in feeling bad because somebody else did. Now I'm not so sure of either. I know that being in the hospital made me selfish. Getting surgeries made me think mainly about whether I'd have to get another one. When bad things happened to other people, I imagined them happening to me. I didn't know if this was empathy or theft.

For example: one September, my brother woke up in a hotel room in Sweden and couldn't move half his face. He was diagnosed with something called Bell's palsy. No one really understands why it happens or how to make it better. The doctors gave him a steroid called prednisone that made him sick. He threw up most days around twilight. He sent us a photo. It looked lonely and grainy. His face slumped. His pupil glistened in the flash, bright with the gel he had to put on his eye to keep it from drying out. He couldn't blink.

I found myself obsessed with his condition. I tried to imagine what it was like to move through the world with an unfamiliar face. I thought about what it would be like to wake up in the morning, in the groggy space where you've managed to forget things, to forget your whole life, and then snapping to, realizing: *yes, this is how things are.* Checking the mirror: still there. I tried to imagine how you'd feel a little crushed, each time, coming out of dreams to another day of being awake with a face not quite your own.

I spent large portions of each day—pointless, fruitless spans of time—imagining how I would feel if my face was paralyzed too. I stole my brother's trauma and projected it onto myself like a magic-lantern pattern of light. I obsessed, and told myself this obsession was empathy. But it wasn't, quite. It was more like *in*pathy. I wasn't expatriating myself into another life so much as importing its problems into my own.

Dave doesn't believe in feeling bad just because someone else does. This isn't his notion of support. He believes in listening, and asking questions, and steering clear of assumptions. He thinks imagining someone else's pain with too much surety can be as damaging as failing to imagine it. He believes in humility. He believes in staying strong enough to stick around. He stayed with me in the hospital, five nights in those crisp white beds, and he lay down with my monitor wires, colored strands carrying the electrical signature of my heart to a small box I held in my hands. I remember lying tangled with him, how much it meant—that he was willing to lie down in the mess of wires, to stay there with me.

In order to help the med students empathize better with us, we have to empathize with them. I try to think about what makes them fall short of what they're asked—what nervousness or squeamishness or callousness—and how to speak to their sore spots without bruising them: the one so stiff he shook my hand like we'd just made a business deal; the chipper one so eager to befriend me she hadn't washed her hands at all.

One day we have a sheet cake delivered for my supervisor's birthday—dry white cake with ripples of strawberry jelly between its layers—and we sit around our conference table eating her cake with plastic forks while she doesn't eat anything at all. She tells us what kind of syntax we should use when we tell the students about bettering their empathy. We're supposed to use the "When . . . felt" frame. *When you forgot to wash your hands, I felt protective of my body. When you told me 11 wasn't on the pain scale, I felt dismissed.* For the good parts also: *When you asked me questions about Will, I felt like you really cared about my loss.*

A 1983 study titled "The Structure of Empathy" found a correlation between empathy and four major personality clusters: sensitivity, nonconformity, even-temperedness, and social self-confidence. I like the word "structure." It suggests empathy is an edifice we build like a home or office—with architecture and design, scaffolding and electricity. The Chinese character for "listen" is built of many parts: the characters for ears and eyes, the horizontal line that signifies undivided attention, the swoop and teardrops of heart.

Rating high for the study's "sensitivity" cluster feels intuitive. It means agreeing with statements like "I have at one time or another tried my hand at writing poetry," or "I have seen some things so sad they almost made me feel like crying," and *dis*agreeing with statements like: "I really don't care whether people like me or dislike me." This last one seems to suggest that empathy might be, at root, a barter, a bid for others' affection: *I care about your pain* is another way to say, *I care if you like me.* We care in order to be cared for. We care because we are porous. The feelings of others matter, they are *like* matter: they carry weight, exert gravitational pull.

It's the last cluster, social self-confidence, that I don't understand as well. I've always treasured empathy as the particular privilege of the invisible, the observers who are shy precisely *because* they sense so much—because it is overwhelming to say even a single word when you're sensitive to every last flicker of nuance in the room. "The relationship between social self-confidence and empathy is the most difficult to understand," the study admits. But its explanation makes sense: social confidence is a prerequisite but not a guarantee; it can "give a person the courage to enter the interpersonal world and practice empathetic skills." We should empathize from courage, is the point—and it makes me think about how much of my empathy comes from fear. I'm afraid other people's problems will happen to me, or else I'm afraid other people will stop loving me if I don't adopt their problems as my own.

Jean Decety, a psychologist at the University of Chicago, uses fMRI scans to measure what happens when someone's brain responds to another person's pain. He shows test subjects images of painful situations (hand caught in scissors, foot under door) and compares these scans to what a brain looks like when its body is actually in pain. Decety has found that imagining the pain of others activates the same three areas (prefrontal cortex, anterior insula, anterior singulate) as experiencing pain itself. I feel heartened by that correspondence. But I also wonder what it's good for.

During the months of my brother's Bell's palsy, whenever I woke up in the morning and checked my face for a fallen cheek, a drooping eye, a collapsed smile, I wasn't ministering to anyone. I wasn't feeling toward my brother so much as I was feeling toward a version of myself—a self that didn't exist but theoretically shared his misfortune.

I wonder if my empathy has always been this, in every case: just a bout of hypothetical self-pity projected onto someone else. Is this ultimately just solipsism? Adam Smith confesses in his *Theory of Moral Sentiments*: "When we see a stroke aimed and just ready to fall upon the leg or arm of another person, we naturally shrink and draw back our own leg or our own arm."

We care about ourselves. Of course we do. Maybe some good comes from it. If I imagine myself fiercely into my brother's pain, I get some sense, perhaps, of what he might want or need, because I think, *I would want this. I would need this.* But it also seems like a fragile pretext, turning his misfortunes into an opportunity to indulge pet fears of my own devising.

I wonder which parts of my brain are lighting up when the med students ask me, *How does that make you feel?* Or which parts of their brains are glowing when I say, *the pain in my abdomen is a ten.* My condition isn't real. I know this. They know this. I'm simply going through the motions. They're simply going through the motions. But motions can be more than rote. They don't just express feeling; they can give birth to it.

Empathy isn't just something that happens to us—a meteor shower of synapses firing across the brain—it's also a choice we make: to pay attention, to extend ourselves. It's made of exertion, that dowdier cousin of impulse. Sometimes we care for another because we know we should, or because it's asked for, but this doesn't make our caring hollow. The act of choosing simply means we've committed ourselves to a set of behaviors greater than the sum of our individual inclinations: *I will listen to his sadness, even when I'm deep in my own.* To say, *going through the motions*—this isn't reduction so much as acknowledgment of effort—the labor, the *motions*, the dance—of getting inside another person's state of heart or mind.

This confession of effort chafes against the notion that empathy should always rise unbidden, that "genuine" means the same thing as "unwilled," that intentionality is the enemy of love. But I believe in intention and I believe in work. I believe in waking up in the middle of the night and packing our bags and leaving our worst selves for our better ones.

Leslie Jamison

Ob-Gyn

SP Training Materials (Cont.)

OPENING LINE: You don't need one. Everyone comes here for the same reason.

PHYSICAL PRESENTATION AND TONE: Wear loose pants. You have been told to wear loose pants. Keep your voice steady and articulate. You are about to spread your legs for a doctor who won't ever know your name. You know the drill, sort of. Act like you do.

ENCOUNTER DYNAMICS: Answer every question like you're clarifying a coffee order. Be courteous and nod vigorously. Make sure your heart stays on the other side of the white wall behind you. If the nurse asks you whether you are sure about getting the procedure, say *yes* without missing a beat. Say *yes* without a trace of doubt. Don't mention the way you felt when you first saw the pink cross on the stick—that sudden expansive joy at the possibility of a child, at your own capacity to have one. Don't mention this single moment of joy because it might make it seem as if you aren't completely sure about what you're about to do. Don't mention this single moment of joy because it might hurt. It will feel—more than anything else does—like the measure of what you're giving up. It maps the edges of your voluntary loss.

Instead, tell the nurse you weren't using birth control but wasn't that silly and now you are going to start.

If she asks what forms of birth control you have used in the past, say condoms. Suddenly every guy you've ever slept with is in the room with you. Ignore them. Ignore the memory of that first time—all that fumbling, and then pain—while Rod Stewart crooned "Broken Arrow" from a boom box on the dresser. *Who else is gonna give you a broken arrow? Who else is gonna give you a bottle of rain?*

Say you used condoms but don't think about all the times you didn't—in an Iowan graveyard, in a little car by a dark river—and definitely don't say why, how the risk made you feel close to those boys, how you courted the incredible gravity of what your bodies could do together.

If the nurse asks about your current partner, you should say, *we are very committed*, like you are defending yourself against some legal charge. If the nurse is listening closely, she should hear fear nestled like an egg inside your certainty.

If the nurse asks whether you drink, say yes to that too. Of course you do. Like it's no big deal. Your lifestyle habits include drinking to excess. You do this even when you know there is a fetus inside you. You do it to forget there is a fetus inside you; or to feel like maybe this is just a movie about a fetus being inside you.

The nurse will eventually ask, *how do you feel about getting the procedure?* Tell her you feel sad but you know it's the right choice, because this seems like the right thing to say, even though it's a lie. You feel mainly numb. You feel numb until your legs are in the stirrups. Then you hurt. Whatever anesthesia comes through the needle in your arm only sedates you. Days later you feel your body cramping in the night—a deep, hot, twisting pain—and you can only lie still and hope it passes, beg for sleep, drink for sleep, resent Dave for sleeping next to you. You can only watch your body bleed like an inscrutable, stubborn object—something harmed and cumbersome and not entirely yours. You leave your body and don't come back for a month. You come back angry.

You wake up from another round of anesthesia and they tell you all their burning didn't burn away the part of your heart that was broken. You come back and find you aren't alone. You weren't alone when you were cramping through the night and you're not alone now. Dave spends every night in the hospital. You want to tell him how disgusting your body feels: your unwashed skin and greasy hair. You want him to listen, for hours if necessary, and feel everything exactly as you feel it—your pair of hearts in such synchronized rhythm any monitor would show it; your pair of hearts playing two crippled bunnies doing whatever they can. There is no end to this fantasy of closeness. *Who else is gonna give you a broken arrow?* You want him to break with you. You want him to hurt in a womb he doesn't have; you want him to admit he can't hurt that way. You want him to know how it feels in every one of your nerve endings: lying prone on the detergent sheets, lifting your shirt for one more cardiac resident, one more stranger, letting him attach his clips to the line of hooks under your breast, letting him print out your heart, once more, to see if its rhythm has calmed.

It all returns to this: you want him close to your damage. You want humility and presumption and whatever lies between, you want that too. You're tired of begging for it. You're tired of grading him on how well he gives it. You want to learn how to stop feeling sorry for yourself. You want to write an essay about the lesson. You throw away the checklist and let him climb into your hospital bed. You let him part the heart wires. You sleep. He sleeps. You wake, pulse feeling for another pulse, and there he is again.

Interview with Leslie Jamison

1. When faced with not knowing how to respond as a medical actor—like when the student doctor asks you about your fake hometown because it was his real hometown—you reverted into cliché behavior in an attempt to stay on-script. When beginning nonfiction writers are telling a half-truth (or they don't know how to write what needs to be written), they also

rely on clichés. What advice do you have for overcoming trite or vague descriptions when writing about secrets, half-truths, and lies?

I often find that it's my most personal pieces that require the most intense revision process—the most drafts, the most rethinking and questioning between drafts—for precisely this reason: the material that's closest is often most vulnerable to the possibility of an overly simplistic telling. With my own life, there are certain incidents or stories where I can feel myself falling into the groove of a familiar version—the version I've told friends, at cocktail parties, what have you—and the revision process asks me to upend this familiar version and get to something more complicated, much messier, instead. So *use* the drafting process—not as a burden or an obstacle, a series of hoops to jump through—but as a liberating opportunity to come back to a story over and over again, an opportunity to peel away its surface and find the tangle underneath. I think with secrets or deeply personal material, the desire to withhold—or not tell the messiest version—can be particularly strong, but that's all the more reason to take refuge in the drafting process. All you are doing is drafting—it's provisional—and that can be quite freeing (it has been for me) with really loaded material.

2. You write that for doctors to learn to treat conversion disorder, "The clinician must excavate a sadness the patient hasn't identified." Does the same go for writers who want to write about secrets? For example, would you ever tell a student, "The writer must excavate a secret the family hasn't identified?"

I absolutely believe in writing—even deeply personal writing—as a process of discovery rather than revelation. I don't write what I already know about myself; I write what I'm in the process of discovering about myself. I often tell students: *write toward mystery.* Which is to say: write towards those parts of your life, those situations or incidents or people from your past, that still seem elusive or mysterious or unexplained to you, that still haunt you because you don't entirely know what to make of them yet. *That* will be the material with real heat, with real energy—that really sings. The question of what to reveal about the lives of others—family secrets or deeply personal material that's shared—is different for every writer, and every situation. I'd advise recklessness in the drafting process and deep carefulness and thoughtfulness in the publishing process—let yourself write what you want to write, but think about what you want to offer to the public eye, and what the price might be—for yourself, for others, for relationships.

3. At the end of the essay, you give us your script for yourself as a standardized patient getting an abortion. How did the frame of "encounter dynamics" influence your process for writing about that day?

The story of this essay is really a story about formal experimentation, and the liberating influence of formal experimentation. I'd written several drafts of this essay that were using my experience as a medical actor to launch into a broader consideration of empathy; but I was only skirting around the edges of my own experiences as a patient. I felt self-conscious about bringing them in, as if they were intruding on the material of the essay. A trusted mentor of mine—the wonderful Charles D'Ambrosio—read a draft of the piece, and told me (in quite gracious and productive terms) that it felt like I was coming up to the brink of something but not yet confronting it. I was backing away. He said that my tone—when I briefly mentioned certain experiences in my own life—felt oddly detached, almost clinical, as if I was turning my own life into one of these scripts. Though he didn't mean it that way (literally), I felt—in his response—the seeds of possibility, the blueprint of a possible experiment: What if I *did* turn my own life into a script? What would that look like? So I did. And it turned out that telling my own story in the form of a dossier was actually quite freeing for me—it gave me a certain amount of distance from my own experience, and allowed me to consider that experience in terms of how it resonated with the big questions of the piece (about relating to the lives and pain of others.) I was able to follow the material because I was glancing at it somewhat obliquely, through this experimental form.

Changing the Subject

Amy E. Robillard

MA'S BECOME OBSESSED WITH THE MISSING BABY TO THE POINT THAT IT'S THE first thing she says when I call, and it's the subject of the very first thing she says to me when I arrive back home in Massachusetts in November. I've told everyone that I'm going home because I want to see her while she still knows who I am. Not that I think she ever really knew who I was.

I walk into the house, the smell of cat and men and old woman assaulting me, the anguish and despair of these walls threatening to crush me as I put my bag down near the kitchen table. Ma sits in her chair at the head of the table. She doesn't get up, so I sit down next to her on the bench with its crusty layers of salt and syrup and diet Coke. Her face is angry, disgusted, agitated. "I don't know why they're not giving the baby back," she spits out. "I'm gonna have to get a lawyer."

I take a deep breath. My heart is racing and I feel shaky all over as I tell her that *I'm* the baby and that I'm fine. I'm right here. I'm forty years old, I tell her. See? I'm fine. You don't have to worry about the baby.

She shakes her head, points her finger at the ceiling, and says, "Don't say anything about the girl. He doesn't believe she's missing." She's referring to my brother Guy, who lives upstairs with his portable fridge and his microwave and his one set of dishes and silverware. He comes downstairs only when he needs to. He's fed up with her stories. He no longer wants to hear about the missing baby.

Michael comes from a good family—parents who care, a younger sister he cares about. I'm intimidated right off by the way they seem to like one another. They seem to like me, too, but I don't trust it. I can't trust it. I know Michael likes me because he's physically affectionate with me, but his parents are another story. Of course they can see right through me, what a bad and ugly person I am deep down.

We have sex for the first time in his bathtub. I learn that it was his first time only later when he writes me a letter telling me so. We're in love, and we have a lot of sex. At my house when nobody's home, at his house when nobody's home, in the park near his house. We lie in his childhood bed fooling around under the covers when his mom knocks on the door and asks us if we want cookies warm from the oven. You can't make this shit up. Even in the books I read moms don't deliver warm cookies to their kids' bedrooms. We'd quickly adjust ourselves to make it look as though we'd just been snuggling and say, sure, we'll have a cookie.

My relationship with Michael is like nothing I've ever experienced. He genuinely seems to love me. My girlfriends probably love me, but there's very little physical affection involved. Hugs are awkward. My girlfriends and I tell each other everything, but the physical closeness I experience with Michael transforms me into a person capable of being loved. I become singularly focused on Michael. All I want to do is be with him because he makes me feel good about myself in ways that nobody has ever done before. He wants to marry me. I want to marry him. We decide we'll name our first daughter Caitlyn.

From my mother I learned to love animals with a desperation that often makes my heart hurt, to fear all of the trouble men could get me in, to be careful what I wished for because I just might get it. And now I'm learning what happens to the stories we're not allowed to tell, what shame does to a person, and the ways we ultimately lose control.

I'm pretty sure I know the exact time it happened. It's just a few weeks before we both go away to different schools. This time it just feels different, like something has changed and there's no going back. It's one of the few times we have sex without protection, and when Michael comes, I feel it. Something just happened. I know it. And the timing of the pregnancy later proves me right. I wish I had said something about it at the time to somebody else so that I wouldn't now seem to be imposing on that event something that wasn't there.

The next day Katie and I have appointments at the Holyoke Planned Parenthood to get on the pill. I'm seventeen; Katie just turned eighteen a few weeks earlier. So nervous on the ride over. "We're not gonna hafta get exams, are we?" I ask.

"No, of course not. They're just gonna give us a prescription."

"Right. We don't need to have an exam for that." Each of us convincing ourselves that we'll be okay, that the rules we're pretty sure apply to everyone else don't apply to us.

We're separated when Katie is called for her appointment first. I sit in the waiting room anxious, trying to imagine what's going to happen next. Picking at my cuticles. Biting my fingernails. Shaking my right leg nearly uncontrollably.

"Amy?" A nurse comes to the waiting room with a file in hand. I stand up. She tells me her name, asks me how I'm doing today.

"Good." I follow her into a very small exam room and note the stirrups right away. Fuck.

"What was the first day of your last period?"

"I'm not sure exactly. Probably around the 6th or 7th."

"Are you on any medications?"

"Nope."

"Have you had unprotected sex in the last two weeks?"

Deep breath. "No." Too ashamed to tell her the truth.

"Okay. We're gonna have you undress from the waist down, including panties. Hop up on the table when you're ready, and cover yourself with this sheet. The doctor will be in in just a few minutes."

Fuck.

Later, in the car, Katie and I don't say much. I don't tell her about last night's sex. I don't tell her about lying to the nurse about last night's sex. The next morning I open the free one-month sample of the pill, knowing, just knowing it's too late.

"I find out tomorrow."

"About what?"

"About the baby. What they've done with her. They're gonna tell me."

"Who is?"

"I don't know. The Brusseaus. They moved to the other town."

Guy tells me that when they're at the grocery store, Ma wants to buy baby food. He steers her toward the cat food instead. A year and a half ago, he called 911 when she became hysterical about the missing baby. "Where's the baby?" she shrieked.

Guy pointed toward Ruby the cat. "You mean Ruby? She's right here."

"No. The baby. Where's the baby?"

"Ma, there is no baby."

"Whaddyou mean there's no baby! Where's the goddamn baby?"

"Do you mean Amy?"

"For chrissakes, no. Where's the baby?" And she began to cry.

That, Guy tells me, was when he knew something was really wrong. He called our oldest brother, Timmy, who lived in the same house, in the basement, and was still sleeping from his second-shift job at the post office. When Timmy didn't answer, Guy called 911.

Timmy later called me from the hospital and told me that Ma had been looking all over for me. "She thinks Guy stole you."

She told us girls over and over again not to have kids until we got married, that she sure as shit wasn't going to take care of any babies, that men were trouble. She told my oldest sister Sue not to go behind the bushes with boys. She told me to marry a rich man, a doctor preferably, but most of all she told me not to have babies until I was married to that rich man.

I've just begun my freshman year at Clark University in Worcester, and Michael's an hour away at Wentworth in Boston. I'm desperate to see him all the time, and the weekends can't get here fast enough. I seriously consider transferring to a school in Boston because I can't bear the thought of being away from him for so long. I'm not living during the week. I'm existing just long enough to get to the weekend so I can see him. He has a car, but I don't, so when it's my turn to go see him, I take the bus. Lisa, a friend from high school who's also at Clark, often gives me a ride to the bus station. I feel sick when he's not around.

For one of his first assignments in his English 101 course, Michael brings in my senior portrait, framed, and delivers a presentation to the class about me.

How we met, how long we've been together, that I want to be a writer, that I love playing Scrabble, that I've had the same best friend since fifth grade. Some of his new friends tease him about it, but he doesn't care.

In early September I begin throwing up. The sight of a stray hair in the sink in the girls' room makes me heave. A stray noodle in the sink, left behind from someone washing their dishes, makes me puke. After a week of this, a store-bought pregnancy test confirms that my hunch is correct. On a weekend when Michael and I are both home in Chicopee, we sit on my bed and I tell him. We hold each other and cry.

There's really never any question about what to do. I'll have an abortion. Neither of us is ready to be a parent, and we've just started college. Back at school in Boston, Michael gets in touch with a counselor on campus to help us sort through what we'll have to do next. She hooks us up with a patient advocate, Laura, whose job it is to help me get an appointment at Planned Parenthood and to help me navigate the court system.

I'll be eighteen on October 20. By that time I'll be into my second trimester. Massachusetts's law says that I need either a parent's permission or a court order in order to get an abortion before I turn eighteen. There's no way Ma will give permission, and I don't really want her to know about this, so we opt for the court route. Laura manages everything and gets us time in front of the judge in Boston.

I'm wearing all blue. I'm not showing yet, but my fantasy is that once the abortion is over, some of my tummy pudge will be gone, too. I'm obsessed with how fat I am.

Michael sits in the jury box with Laura. I sit in the witness box while the judge asks me a series of questions designed to help him determine if I'm mature enough to make this decision without my parents.

"Is your boyfriend here with you today?"

"Yes." I point to him. "Here he is."

"Does your boyfriend agree with this decision?"

"Yes."

"Do you have a place in mind for the procedure?"

"Yes. The Planned Parenthood in Brookline."

"When will you turn eighteen?"

"On October 20. But if we wait that long, it'll be a more complicated procedure."

"Why can't you tell your mother?"

"She's pro-life, your Honor, and I know she won't give me permission."

The judge rules that I'm fit to make this decision for myself, especially given how close I am to my eighteenth birthday. We make the appointment. Michael withdraws the four hundred dollars from his savings account.

"You know I have a baby, don't you?"

"No."

"Oh Christ. You don't know? She's about four or five now."

I talk with my therapist about how best to respond to moments like these. Do I go along with her and pretend that there is a baby, that the baby's okay, and that she shouldn't worry? Or do I just keep changing the subject the way I have been, telling her about taking the dogs swimming or about the latest funny thing that one of them has done? Should I tell her about the squirrel Essay and the neighbor dog killed last week?

He tells me that the best thing to do is probably to ask her what she's most worried about. If she's worried about the baby's safety, tell her that from what you know, the baby's just fine. If she's worried about her own role in losing the baby, tell her that you know she did her best.

Two weeks before my eighteenth birthday, Michael and I take the T to Planned Parenthood in Brookline. We sit together silently in the waiting room until my name is called. I go back alone, change into a hospital gown, and sit on an exam table and wait. The doctor and two nurses come in. Someone administers a sedative, and the nurse holding my hand asks me to talk to her about where I work.

"At school, just filing and stuff."

"Filing, huh? Secretarial, then?"

"Yeah." Woozy now. Can no longer engage in conversation. I don't feel a thing. Afterwards, the nurse helps me put on my panties but not before adhering an enormously thick maxi pad to them.

"You're going to bleed a lot. You'll need thick pads for a few days."

I nod. She leads me out to the recovery area, where I drink ginger ale and eat crackers and sleep for I don't know how long. Michael's there with me. He holds me tight.

Does the time come for everyone when holding it in just won't do anymore? I kept the story of my abortion to myself until Michael broke up with me two years later. I told all my friends about it and I didn't feel judged. I felt, instead, the kind of empathy I'd been seeking by telling them in the first place. And I've told the story to friends since that time, but mostly the way I've told this story is by steadfastly defending a woman's right to choose. As a teacher of rhetoric, I make it a point to use public discourse about abortion as an example of a controversy that remains in stasis because of both parties' unwillingness to concede the terms of the debate. One side talks about choice, the other side talks about a baby's life, and until both sides decide they're talking about the same thing, the controversy will rage on.

During my visit home, I ask Ma what she wanted to be when she was a kid. She can't remember or she doesn't know or maybe she never really wanted to be anything. Just whatever happened to her: that was her life. And now as she worries about her missing baby and wants others to hear her, we can't. It's not right, this story, so nobody believes her, and because nobody believes her, she's doomed to repeat it and repeat it until somebody does.

A few weeks later, Michael calls me at school. He's crying. "They know," he tells me.

"Whaddyou mean, *they know*?"

"My mom called me because she saw the withdrawal from my bank account. She pressured me into telling her."

"Jeeeeezus."

"They thought I was doing drugs, that I'd used the money to buy drugs. I had to tell them."

"You *didn't* have to tell them."

If before this I'd been sure that Michael's parents didn't like me, I was certain now that they hated me. I knew how they felt about abortion. They gave money to pro-life organizations. I'd aborted their first grandchild. They were now looking back on that night they picked us up in Boston to drive us home to Chicopee. It was the night I'd had the abortion. I lay in the back seat on Michael's lap, claiming that the moaning was just from cramps. Now they knew the pain I'd been moaning about.

I'm not sure I ever looked either of them in the eye again. I rarely went to Michael's house when we were home from school, and when I did, I'd stay in the car or keep whatever conversation I was forced to have with his parents to small talk. This wasn't their information to know. I felt so betrayed by them. My body. My decision. My choice to keep it to myself. But they didn't let me do that.

Michael later told me that his dad had told *him* that when his mom first saw the bank statement, the first thing she said was that she knew I'd had an abortion.

Ma's official dementia diagnosis came last summer after an appointment with a specialist. Timmy took her to the appointment and only later found out that the fourth person in the room was there because Timmy was being investigated on charges of elder abuse. As it happened, Ma's friend Betty reported him for taking away Ma's license, for taking all her money, and for threatening to kill her and the cat. Every time Ma saw Betty, she'd say the same things, so Betty figured there must be something going on and she'd better report Timmy to the authorities. The charges were of course dropped, and Timmy, to his credit, was able to see the situation from Betty's perspective. "She was trying to be a good friend," he tells me. I marvel at his patience and he tells me he's just worn out. He worries that he's on the verge of a nervous collapse.

Ma calls me one Saturday night, and as soon as I see her name on my phone I worry that she's dead. Ma doesn't call me. I call her. Ma doesn't ask how I'm doing. I ask her.

I pick up the phone. She's agitated. "He's gonna kill the cat."

"Who?"

"That man."

"Do you mean Timmy?"

"Yes, Timmy. He's going to kill us all!"

"Oh, Mum, he's not. He loves you."

"He's trying to take my kids away from me."

"Nobody's trying to do that. We're all fine."

"Then why is he trying to take the baby?"

"I promise you he's not trying to take the baby."

"Sometimes I think he doesn't like me anymore."

For a number of years when I was in my teens, Ma worked at a factory in Holyoke making kaleidoscopes. She'd bring home small kaleidoscopes for us to look through, to turn slowly as we held them up to our eyes, watching our world shift and refract and multiply.

Ma hasn't been allowed to tell her own stories because the fear she has felt—the fear she felt earlier, when she was young, the fear of shame—has sedimented her ability to tell. In order for her to be able to tell her stories of loss, she'd have to pull them up from that deep, dark place where they've gone to grow and to infect (and inflect) her whole self. Pulling them up takes a whole heck of a lot of work—the kind of work she's never been taught to do, the kind of work she's never felt safe enough to do. And so her stories of trauma and her stories of grief fester inside her, and when she's tired or agitated or just plain old and suffering from dementia, they find their way out, but they're jumbled up. They became broken, rearranged in the excavation.

When she brings up the baby and we try to change the subject, her mouth sets into a wrinkled line and I watch her eyes shift from fear to anger to resignation. Our eyes don't meet for long. She turns away and shakes her head in disgust.

Twenty years later, Michael and I get back in touch through Facebook. After the night he told me his father knew about the abortion, we never talked about it again. Now, I ask him how many people he's told.

It's not who, though, that matters, but *how* he told the story. "I'm not proud of this but I think it's important for you to know this about me. Even though there really was no question of what the decision was going to be for us, I have always told the story as though it was a very difficult decision. I guess if nothing else to come across as not being heartless to those with different beliefs."

I forget, sometimes, that my abortion story is not mine alone. I forget, sometimes, that so many who might hear my story would shame me. Michael anticipated that shame and created a story in which our decision was a difficult one.

The day after Ma called me that Saturday, I called my Aunt Judy, Ma's younger sister. "Is there *anything* I don't know about Ma that would help me understand the persistence of this missing baby story?" Judy hesitated. "There is one thing, but it happened a long time ago and I'm not sure she'd want you kids to know."

Fearful that what Judy knew might make me even more depressed about my mother, I told her that I wanted to know *only if* she thought it would help.

"There was a baby that was taken away, but it was by choice. When your mother was a teenager, she had a boyfriend that she was totally in love with. Things happened. She got pregnant, and our parents sent her away to have the baby. I was just a kid, you know there's nine years between us, and I didn't know where she'd gone. The neighbor girl kept asking me where my sister went and I had to tell her I didn't know! I don't think she believed me. Eventually Mom and Dad had to tell me."

There *was* a baby. My mother was sent away in shame to give birth to a child who was then taken from her. Judy says Ma knew that Judy knew, but they never once talked about it. "Do you think she talked to *anyone* about it?" I ask Judy.

"I really have no idea. I doubt it."

When I tell Guy what I've learned, the first thing he says is, "There's another one of us out there? Poor thing."

My therapist advises me not to talk with Ma about the baby. This is information meant only to help us understand her obsession with the baby. She's not crazy, after all. She got pregnant as a teenager and had no choice but to give birth and give the baby up. She's never told the story. Instead she buried it. The loss of that baby shaped most everything she did and said to us kids, surely. She learned that with pregnancy comes loss, that with telling comes shame.

Timmy: "She never wanted to have kids."

Guy: "She wanted *babies*. She loved babies. She just hates it when they grow up."

Back then people didn't go to therapists for things like this, Judy tells me. Back then you were just a whore.

In *Aftermath: Violence and the Remaking of a Self*, Susan Brison suggests that "Perhaps there is a psychological imperative, analogous to the legal imperative, to keep telling one's story until it is heard. After the story has been heard and acknowledged, one can let it go, or unfreeze it. One can unclench."

Ma can never unclench. Her demented mind is like the kaleidoscopes she brought home for us when we were teenagers: it shifts and refracts and multiplies that baby born more than sixty years ago to the point that she's unrecognizable to us all.

Interview with Amy Robillard

1. What was the hardest part of this essay to get right?

I'm not sure there was a hardest part, but I'll say a little bit about what prompted me to write it. I'd long since shed any sense of shame about the abortion, and I'd written the story about Michael and me long before I'd learned about my mother's teenage pregnancy. I thought that the fact that we'd had to go to court to get permission from a judge, that the timing of the abortion two weeks before my eighteenth birthday, and the terrible timing of going for birth control the day after the night I'm pretty sure the baby was conceived—all of these things in themselves made for a good essay. But I didn't do anything with it because I wasn't confident enough about my writing to send it anywhere. Then in the summer of 2013 I learned about my mother's first baby and I was stunned. That news made me rethink so many things, just one of them being the story of my abortion. It occurred to me that my mother and I had both gotten pregnant as teenagers, but we'd had such different choices available to us, such different narratives. All of my mother's stories about the baby suddenly made a different kind of sense and I knew I had a different kind of essay here. I knew that I could combine my mother's story with the abortion story to make something good.

2. In Michael's telling of the lead-up to the abortion, he uses the phrase "difficult decision," which is wording you then reflect on. What he says is not a complete lie, nor is it a half-truth, exactly. What is it, and why is it important for creative nonfiction writers to distinguish between these subtleties?

The reason I included that part about Michael's telling of the story is that part of what surprised me when we got back in touch was not that he had told people—of course he had—but that he had been so rhetorically savvy about it. I think that because I hadn't talked with him in so long, I'd forgotten what kind of person he was—kind, gentle, sensitive, thoughtful, caring—and he was still that kind of person and had been all along. Time makes us forget. So when he told the story of the abortion to others, he took their feelings into account and didn't want to offend what might be their very different views on the issue. Of course it wasn't a difficult decision for us. What Michael provided was a polite lie.

3. Many essays about abortion find their urgency in details about the actual procedure. However, one of the strongest scenes here seems to be the brief appearance in the courtroom, which is dramatic even though it's heavy on routine judicial language. What advice do you have for writers who want to compose compelling scenes about divisive political issues that also overlap with a personal secret?

Honestly, that courtroom scene is my least favorite because it's so dry. I almost cut it. If I'd had more time with the essay, I probably would have. It reveals important details about the experience, but I sort of hate it *as writing*. I don't find it compelling at all. So I guess my advice would be to allow yourself to write through what seems dry and deadly but ultimately reveals an important social truth. I went to court because I knew on some level that my mother would not give me permission to have an abortion. I didn't know anything about her own experience with her teenage pregnancy. I just knew that she was pro-life and that no amount of convincing would have persuaded her.

4. All over the world, secrets about sex, pregnancy, and their social consequences get kept but also discreetly told across generations, often female to female. Do you think that publishing the full truth about your secret (and your mother's secret) will help our culture not feel the need to keep such secrets? Have you received any reactions to the essay that you could share with us here?

That's a big question. I'm not sure my one story can have that kind of impact, but I think that the accumulation of stories like mine can begin to have that kind of impact. When I teach essays and memoir, I always paraphrase a Francine Prose observation that memoir always tells two stories: the first is the story you're reading and the second is the story that the writer has made it, has survived long enough and well enough to *write* the story you're holding in your hands. With stories about abortion, the stakes of that second story are particularly high. In a September 2015 piece on *Salon*, Valerie Tarico writes that "Far too often, the fight about abortion focuses on the procedure or surrounding circumstances instead of the empowered life that follows." She wants to shift the focus to what comes after the abortion, years after. "The prudence or wisdom of an abortion may be obvious at the time, but the power and the full meaning of that decision only begin to come into focus in the years and decades that follow." The very fact that I was able to *write* this essay and to have it published on *The Rumpus* and republished here in this anthology is evidence that the abortion was the right decision. Too often the focus is on what percentage of women regret or don't regret their abortion some number of years later. What about the number of women who honestly rarely think about them? What about the number of women who, because of that abortion, have been able to build rich, meaningful lives teaching and writing and living and loving in relatively unremarkable ways? We don't get surveyed. It was the right thing to do. But there's also a defensiveness that comes with saying that too much and I don't want to go there either. I think just living my life and letting my story speak for itself while neither hiding nor broadcasting the abortion is the best way to have what I hope is at least a small impact on others who may be hesitant to share their stories.

S-Turns

Jon Pineda

THE SUMMER AFTER MY SISTER DIED WE DROVE SOUTH ON NC HWY 12 TO
S-Turns, a known surfing spot just after the weathered station near Pea Island
Wildlife Reserve on the Outer Banks.

Coming off the huge, sun-bleached bridge there at Oregon Inlet, you could see
the upheaval of water below, its faint white lines like minced coke on a mirrored
surface. My friend Robinson drove. Ian Astbury, lead singer of The Cult, wailed,
Hollow man . . . Hollow man.

I cranked the volume.

Along the road's shoulder was a row of beaters, mostly Hondas and Datsuns,
with the black rubber straps of their surf racks already undone, stirring in the
offshore breeze.

The locals, mostly roofing contractors, had stopped their work on nearby cot-
tages and were skipping out to spend the day in the swell. Their trucks, scarred
beds filled with planks of salt-treated timbers and pallets of bundled shingles,

were wedged in intervals within the same line of cars. Everything gave off the appearance of having been abandoned.

Robinson pulled in behind a group of guys with angry mops of blond hair, tangled towheads most of them, spewing clouds of pale smoke. Some were eagerly yanking down squash-tailed thrusters.

I leaned forward and braced my hands on the cracked blue upholstery of the dashboard, smacking at it, as if the car would halt suddenly from this gesture of erratic drumming. Billy Duffy's guitar licks swirled in a bright mixture of chorus and delay effects pedals.

Easy on the Fairmont Testa Rossa, bra, Robinson said, his eyes already bloodshot. It was a joke he liked to use.

One of the towheads crouched to rub a fresh skin of wax over the deck of his In the Eye. Others started darting across the road and charged the dune ahead, freeing themselves of the insults thrown furiously by the one left behind.

Even then, you could see the boundaries of clouds through the cracked windshield, the collision of sky gray causing the hulls of each to dimple and sink into the next. By the time we both made it over the dune ourselves, the giant rigging coasted overhead. But it didn't matter.

We slid down into the trough of sand, smearing deep footprints left by the overzealous, and stared ahead at what had garnered such excitement.

Man, it's going *off*, Robinson crowed, and crouched to attach the Velcro anklet of his leash, but I was already running, my legs spinning and then nothing, stillness as I lifted and flew to spear the face of the oncoming shore break with the nose of my board, a Wave Riding Vehicles that had been locally shaped.

Another wave was waiting for me, and I ducked it, and when I surfaced, I coughed and then paddled as hard as I could. Robinson came up alongside me and laughed. His hair was dripping down past his chin, brushing the glaze of ocean over the bumps of wax. Almost got caught *inside*, he said, and I nodded.

It was summer. I was almost seventeen. A part of me felt invincible, but you would think it would be the other way around. I carried a death in my head. Everyone I saw in the lineup that day was a ghost. My sister was dead.

By the time Robinson and I had made it to the outside, the storm had assembled into an armada. It sounds stupid to say it this way, but it's how I felt then. Clouds fired rounds of lightning into the endless sets of waves. Streaks whistling like cannonballs.

The first bolts were hitting farther south, in an electric haze where the Hatteras Lighthouse was lost to distance. But you could feel the charge in the air. The hairs on my arms lifted some.

Robinson had taken off on a left and was going backside down the line when he disappeared, getting covered up briefly just before the section jacked up on the inside. Then he was gone for good.

When I paddled over to the break, I spotted a kid I knew from sixth grade. I hadn't seen him in probably five years. So much had already changed in our lives. I didn't remember his name, only that he and I, at the end of that school year, had been in a play together. I remember he had the part of a cat, his whiskers drawn on with mascara by our drama teacher, and had to spend most of the time on his hands and knees sliding around the dusty stage. Black construction paper triangles made up his ears. We had to perform a few numbers. Most of the play revolved around us: *Dick Whittington and His Cat.*

When he stood up during one of our scenes, he towered over me. The audience, made up of mostly parents, laughed and whistled. What was worse was that we had to do some kind of dance and sing a song. I remember looking at him and singing the line "Anything for you."

Now we both started paddling for the same wave, though he was in better position. He glared at me, and I glared back. For a moment, I wondered if he remembered me.

I pulled back and let him go. He, too, disappeared.

At one point, I was the only surfer on the outside. Lightning fell around me, but I didn't want to go in. The sky lit again and fractured. Anyone who was serious about living this way of life stayed out there. I could see Robinson paddling back out. I could see the boy I used to know doing the same thing. Before they reached me, I took off on a left and stalled a bit on a bottom turn so that I would slow, pulling back, and the wave would cover me.

I mention all of this so that I might reach, again, the hollowness inside. I ran my hand along the face of it. It felt like a secret room. I crouched as the space began to collapse. It happened slowly.

I can still see bits of the sky.

Interview with Jon Pineda

1. In what ways do you see your minimalist narrative as a form for conveying a difficult secret? Also, space is important in your essay. Can you discuss mental and physical spaces in your essay?

The lyrical essay feels so spacious to me. There are lots of places for a difficult secret to hide. Visually, the numerous sections in "S-Turns" are like sets of waves. They roll across the surface of the page and, ultimately, finish into its white space. As for the world within the essay, an infinite number of spaces exist, of course, but it is the "secret" that creates structure, that makes the surrounding thoughts and images more defined. But the "secret" is also held by the narrator (myself) and eventually carried into a "barrel" (that hollow space of a wave folding over), where it resides in both a defined and infinite space.

2. You mention an important song in this lyrical essay, "Hollow Man" by The Cult, and you link it to the hollow space a surfer finds when he rides a wave, as well as the hollowness you feel in loss. Readers familiar with the lyrics of the song will relate, but readers unfamiliar with the song might be left out of the full "secret." So, it's a risk to include it. What advice can you give for beginning writers who want to share but also keep secret a specific piece of music in creative nonfiction?

All writers, beginning or otherwise, should trust their intuition. Add what feels right and remove what feels right. There is the world of the essay, and yet, the essay is also held by everything that isn't included within it.

3. *Dick Whittington and His Cat* is an interesting choice for a school play. Can you discuss the plot in a bit more detail, if you remember it? Also, how do you see the costar of the play as an actor in your narrative? In other words, can you explain why you chose to include him and the peculiar title of the play?

I remember he was an orphan, and he lived on the streets of London. I think that's part of the plot, though I'm not 100 percent certain. I wanted to include the costar of the play because *one*, the boy was there that day in the ocean, and *two*, it hadn't been long after the two of us had performed the play together in the sixth grade that my sister's car accident would occur and our lives would change. To see this boy after having not seen him for years seemed more than a coincidence. As for the play's title, I wanted to include it because it seemed the furthest thing from The Cult and the surf culture that I adored. On one end was who I had been, a boy content to learn lines from a play and sing and dance, unabashed in front of an audience, and on the other end was the person I had become, changed, challenging what it meant to be alive, more introspective. Both versions were framed in half-truths and secrets.

4. Are there "s-turns" in creative nonfiction?

Yes, they're the moments when the creative nonfiction writer moves and exists (albeit temporarily) outside the confines of conventional narrative. The truth of the moment centers the narrative, keeps trying to pull everything back, but the "s-turns" are the imbalance, the necessary sway.

5. Why did you leave the cause of your sister's death out of the essay?

That she had died and that I (the narrator) kept her death a secret in that one instance seemed more important than revealing the specifics of her death. It still does.

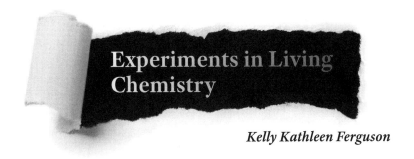

Experiments in Living Chemistry

Kelly Kathleen Ferguson

THE FIRST MORNING AFTER MY LAST DAY OF FIFTH GRADE, MOM INFORMED me that my summer vacation and girlhood were over.

Me: reading *A Wrinkle in Time* in my room, hoping to pull a Meg Murry and tesseract to another planet.

Mom (with a cursory knock while opening the door): "Great news! You get to attend those Summer Enrichment Seminars you enjoyed so much last year. And you can wear"—she pointed with her thin, well-manicured finger at the second drawer of my white dresser—"*your little bra.*"

That was how she pronounced those words, *italicized*, the final "ahhh" birthing in slow motion as it burrowed like a parasite. I ignored her. She smiled and shut the door, knowing I didn't think this news was great at all; I was going to be shuttled off to a glorified babysitting venue against my will, and the two pink pop-up tents on my chest could no longer be ignored.

I stared with great intent at my book, praying that Mrs. Who, Mrs. Which, and Mrs. Whatsit would come for me, after which Calvin O'Keefe would remove my glasses, see past my frizzy hair and braces to the real, beautiful me, where my oddball quirks increased my charm.

I pointedly avoided the drawer where the dreaded white-eyelet garment lurked. Inside, straps crisscrossed over a tiny pink rose, cups padded with wisps of cotton to puff the nipple buds into a shape. A video at school had warned me that I might need one of these someday, a training bra. The word conjured images of Wheaties box champions, teams of preteen girls racing, arms outstretched, as they competed for Olympic breasts.

The pink rose didn't fool me.

Sure, I was in training. Training for hell.

The first day of the Summer Enrichment Seminars I lucked out. Mom enrolled in summer school, so Dad would be driving me. No way would Dad confront me about anything to do with undergarments. That morning I insisted on wearing my yellow rain slicker to cover myself, even though it was July in Alabama.

"I'll *freeze* in there," I insisted. I had a point. Southerners, in retaliation against the heat, generally keep their interiors the temperature of a meat locker.

Dad gave me a sideways glance but he didn't argue. We drove in silence. I didn't even whine about why I had to attend more school right after regular school was out. I hated the constant shuttling about, and many of these so-called educational events were suspect. One time, my mother enrolled me in a baton twirling class—held inside a trailer. And all the coach did was yell at us while she ate McDonald's. After that, I begged my father to let me stay at home. But then he dropped this on me: "Boy, when I was a kid I sure wish I could have done all this great stuff."

Dad had grown up in a cold, grimy Catholic orphanage in Buffalo, New York, and there was just no arguing with that. He had scrounged and strived so I could live the pampered life of a middle-class ingrate. Still, I'm guessing Dad never had to Fancy Strut in front of a former soy bean queen who yelled, "Glimmer, little glo worm! Glimmer!" between bites of her Big Mac.

All I am saying is this: if you are going to eat, you should bring enough for everyone.

I was plunked on the curb of Holt Elementary with a bologna sandwich in a rumpled paper bag and a Chronicle of Narnia stashed in my shorts. I filtered inside with the other nerds of Tuscaloosa County. We were handed a regimen ranging from Life Sciences to Macramé, and dutifully marched to our classrooms so we could become enriched, like flour. The seminars were for "gifted" children, those of us who had passed some third grade Mensa quiz that made sure we never got to spend our summers hanging out at the pool or skipping rocks.

Our first activity of the day was Dramatic Arts, which was held in the gym. When I put on my slicker that morning I had counted on the usual Alabama indoor arctic blast. The gym was a sauna. Within a minute I had mortifying armpit stains and removing the slicker wasn't an option. Soon, sweat began to drip down my back. I waited in dread for one of the odd looks directed at my slicker to become an outright accusation. At some point I knew some loud-mouthed girl (there was always a loud-mouthed girl) would shout, "Why are you wearing that stupid jacket?" while everyone stared and I stammered through some lie. I carefully shifted around to keep myself a moving target. To my relief, this teacher was the bossy kind who left no room for chitchat or humiliation.

The woman's hair was albino blonde drawn back in a severe bun. She wasn't old or young. She didn't wear makeup or speak with a Southern accent. Her thin lips like a slash said there was *a special treat* in store for all of us. We would get to perform *Macbeth*. She informed us she was *a real live* director from the Alabama Shakespeare Festival who was going to help us perform a modified version of the play. We came to understand this woman was no ordinary educator and we were *very fortunate* to have her. This opportunity would be an *experience*.

We tried to look impressed even though we had no idea what she was talking about.

"Shakespeare was a great playwright!" shouted Norvin Richards, a scrawny dweeblet who came up to my neck. Norvin was a tow-headed philosophy professor's son with glasses held around his head by an elastic band.

The director dutifully acknowledged Norvin's superior knowledge, which fired the geek cadre into life. We were all used to being number one in our classrooms, but now all the number ones were gathered together. Who was number one now? We didn't know anything about the Great Bard, but we were familiar enough with school plays to know that someone would get to be the star. The director furrowed her brows for a minute before she arranged us in groups. Then she stood back, hand on hip, scrutinized, frowned, and rearranged us again. This second grouping appeased her. I was moved to the back. The slicker stuck to my skin where her hand cinched my forearm.

With a heavy sigh (*Oh! Woe! Why had she agreed to this?*) the director handed out scripts and explained how things would be: there wasn't much time, and this wasn't how a theatre was usually run, but she would make do. We were not to *roughhouse* around the stage props, which were *very generously* on loan. Auditions would be held at our next meeting. The performance would be held in two weeks.

It wasn't too hard to figure out that if the name of the play was *Macbeth*, then the female lead was Lady Macbeth. While the director paced and lectured I took inventory of the competition. These girls with bony limbs and terrycloth onesies weren't of the sleek blow-dryer tribe from public school. One girl with a freckle-smeared face adjusted her scoliosis brace. Another bent to scratch her scabs. No gleaming, tanned, tube-topped cheerleaders here. I had a shot. The Norvin kid poked my arm. A shot of panic ran through me. I had almost made it through the day unnoticed.

"Hey, lemme tell you a secret," he said.

I bent down. He cupped his hand over his mouth, leaned into me, and belched.

Our last enrichment of the day was Living Chemistry. Within a minute we were all in the thrall of Miss Bussian, a college chemistry student with honey-blonde hair, tan skin, and a mesmerizing Aztec skirt. The despair of our lost summer vacation melted in a desire to merge with her orange-blossom scent. She loved us each the best, we could tell.

Miss Bussian gave us each a Petri dish and a sterile cotton swab. We were instructed to lightly touch a surface, and then lightly touch the agar, and see what grew on the special medium. Just like real scientists!

Being the enriched child I was, I gripped my swab and overanalyzed the situation. I had already bombed Life Science earlier that day. While everyone else *oohed* and *ahhed* over the paramecium flagella in their microscopes, I had faked fascination over a water bubble. The pressure of redemption weighed heavy. This was my chance to make visible the microscopic, to reveal an object's true nature. Everyone else seemed confident as they ran around the room, dabbing the aquarium or the pencil sharpener, but every time I started to make a move, I froze. I mean, who really cared to reveal the inner spirit of a crayon?

Then I thought of something I wanted to know more about.

I snuck the swab into the bathroom, locked the door, pulled down my shorts, and performed a preteen version of a pap smear. I slipped back in the classroom, stealthily lifted the glass lid, touched the cotton end the exact way I was instructed, and sealed the dish.

"Out, damn spot! Out, I say!" I practiced in my closet to escape parental scrutiny. If I tried to add intensity, I only sounded shrill. Mostly I sounded drab, put to shame by the dramatic skills of the housewife who mourned "those dirty rings" on her husband's shirts, before she discovered the delights of Spray 'n Wash. For the sake of High Art the word "damn" had been approved for minors, but it stuck in my craw. Raised in the Bible Belt, I just couldn't shout a curse word. As I tried to project "How tender 'tis to love the babe that milks me," I knew the word "milks" was gross somehow, causing me to fumble.

Yet I persevered. My desire for the female lead was rooted in a long history of frustration. As an early puberizer who had always been tall for her age, I had always been assigned male parts in school plays.

In first grade all the girls were sunflowers, except me—the tree.

In the play about a cavity, I was the dentist.

In *Charlotte's Web* I played Fern's father, Mr. Arable. For my big moment I got to waddle on stage in overalls, slop Wilber, and shout, "That's one terrific pig!"

In our fifth-grade production of *Broadway Musicals* I lip-synced "Go Greased Lighting" in a mechanic's suit.

I was determined to break my long string of roles performed in drag, so in my closet I persisted. I knew my voice was wrong. I didn't sound like a Scottish queen driven to psychosis, but the *blah blah* of a *Peanuts* character with a southern twang. But I had experienced transformation again and again in my piles of books, so technically, I knew the experience was possible. Everyone knew it took the pressure of a real challenge to forge greatness.

That next day the director shouted our roles while we squirmed. My heart thudded as the bit parts were doled out. Eventually, there were no female parts left except Lady Macbeth, and I allowed myself a giddy whiff of hope until—"Kelly Ferguson! Macduff, loyal Thane of Fife."

I didn't even get to be a Weird Sister, and worse, I had a *wife*. Lady Macduff and I avoided eye contact. Ashley Phelps, a willowy girl with blond hair, freckles, and a soft voice was awarded the prize role. She squealed for joy and we all hated her.

One look at the director, already back to grabbing people by the elbow, made me realize it was no use complaining. For our first read-through I wandered Birnam Wood (potted banana trees) with Macbeth, Norvin Richards. As the director went to work on the Weird Sisters we giggled and roughhoused with the props. That we were not supposed to touch anything made wearing the helmets and scurrying around all the more awesome.

In Living Chemistry, Ms. Bussian told us to check on our Petri dishes.

"Don't be disappointed if you don't see much," she said. "It can take up to a few weeks."

We had labeled our dishes so everyone could keep them straight. Needless to say I had no intention of writing "My Vagina" with black marker on a piece of masking tape, so I wrote "Inside Desk" instead.

Despite everyone's excited swabbing, most kids only had a few dark specks, while most had nothing at all—Special Class once again specializing in the mundane. But in the back, one disc emerged from the wash of spotted beige. Encased in glass, a black furry caterpillar crawled across its dish.

"Wow," said Miss Bussian. "That's really something."

She checked the label and looked at me askance, but no way was I telling. Everyone gathered around the dish and gawked. I worried that Ms. Bussian, a science expert, would know vagina growth when she saw it, and that I would be outed somehow for cheating. Given the creature coming to life in the Petri dish, perhaps I should have been more worried about personal hygiene. God knows what that swab picked up from the Holt Elementary bathroom. But health was a small sacrifice to pay for glory. I found myself pleased as Miss Bussian examined the dish in the fluorescent light.

My macramé bracelet was crooked. I still only saw water bubbles in Life Science. The more I tried to project in Shakespeare, the more my atonal voice matched my limp cardboard sword. But in Living Chemistry, I was a star. As the weeks passed, other kids had blotches, smatterings, maybe a little gray fuzz. An unfortunate few, like Lady Macbeth, still had nothing (ha!), her surface blank.

Miss Bussian tried to interest us in the periodic table, and she brought in some liquid nitrogen, which was pretty cool, but really we all just wanted to see what was growing in our Petri dishes, or, more to the point, what was growing in *my* Petri dish. By the end of the week the caterpillar had morphed into a baby hamster surrounded by tornado funnels dervishing in the air.

"Dude!" said Norvin Richards in admiration, whose beige slab sported only an unimpressive smudge.

The day of the play it was time once more for me to don male drag. My mother slicked back my long hair with Dep gel. I was allowed to wear makeup, but only base and extra eyebrow pencil, not eye shadow or lipstick. The true horror of my situation emerged when I put on my costume—tights with a man's white shirt (my father's) worn over the top and belted. The shirt, though, came up too short for comfort and was transparent. With my mother involved, there was no avoiding another debut—*the little bra.*

Today girls can opt for a training bra that is more like a little tank top—the Velcro version of shoelaces. In the seventies, bra training was more serious. We were thrown into the deep end of adjusting straps that dug into our shoulders. We trained for discomfort, for how to adopt a constant half-smile when in fact we were freaking out over the elastic strangling our torsos. We trained for the telltale straps that everyone could see through our blouses, and how to maneuver our arms so we could hook and unhook the back. The "wiggle in" technique worked for the novices, where we assembled the gear, stepped in, and shimmied up. All this training supposedly existed for the purposes of modesty, but these bras only seemed to highlight the two chest beacons that would forever define a part of how we would be perceived as women.

When I shuffled out of my room in my Scottish warrior garb, my parents' hands slapped over their mouths, trying to disguise their mirth. My overall look was completed by a pair of old moccasins, making me a dead ringer for the last pirate Mohican. My parents had just pulled it together when I reached for my sword wrapped in aluminum foil.

"Lead—on—Macduff," Dad sputtered, and they fell over again, wheezing and gasping with tears glittering cruelly on their cheeks. I ran back to my room and slammed the door. No way was I going to be in that *damn* play. Although eventually my Catholic heritage of guilt and duty kicked in as my parents reminded me of my responsibilities. When they wanted pictures, however, I balked. No gruff voices, guilt trips, or sighs from Dad could make me budge on this point. I didn't care what sort of selfish, ungrateful wretch I was.

"She's feeling *sensitive*, Patrick," Mom said, the corners of her mouth twitching, and all I can say is it's a good thing that sword was fake.

At the auditorium, Lady Macbeth was in full regalia. She wore an empire-waist lavender gown with floating gauzy layers, her blonde hair piled in a medieval topknot with ribbons. We thanes and witches choked with envy. I looked around to discover that all the other Scottish warriors at least had a real tunic and real tights. My tights were not tights but support hose—I looked as though I had forgotten my pants. Now I was angry. Not only had I been miscast, I had parents who would rather be thrifty than make sure their daughter didn't look like a complete idiot. Perhaps some of my own Scottish ancestry kicked in; I was ready to go onstage and kick some serious Elizabethan ass.

While internal pep talks and personal belief are the cornerstones of children's literature, they're best left to those with the ability to tesseract across outer space, a skill I would soon pray for. Once I had been given the part of Macduff, I had lost interest in the play, goofing around with Norvin Richards during rehearsals and reading Madeleine L'Engle books at home. I hadn't learned my lines. When it was time to take the stage, I had absolutely no idea what to say.

Terrified my shirt would fly up, I minced across the stage as I kept my sword clutched by my side, shoulders hunched to hide my *little* bra. I patched together pieces of dialogue, hoping to mask my botched lines, but the hot white lights and auditorium of staring parents did nothing to help. My tepid storming of Dunsinane Castle had the texture of Velveeta. The bird-chested Norvin Macbeth could barely lift his sword. My brawny guns, strong from after-school activities and fueled by resentment, made the outcome of the duel a gimme, my execution perfunctory as I splatted the corrupt king to the ground in one swat, thereby killing whatever there might have been of a crush as well.

Tomorrow?

Nobody thought so, not three times, not even once.

My one consolation was that all the enriched kids bombed. Lady Macbeth wailed through her soliloquy with wretched melodrama. The Weird Sisters were depressingly normal, hunched, and giggling through all the best lines. As thanes flung fake mutton at one another, I wondered if anyone had really ever seen a paramecium in Life Science. The director spent the performance running around and hissing lines. Her hair pulled tighter and tighter, causing her expression to resemble a botched face-lift. Banquo's ghost was the only success. His comedic interpretation, a brilliant improv in which he "did the Hustle" around the banquet table, brought the performance to life. At curtain call we shuffled out hangdog to take our bows, but Banquo sprang to the front, arms outstretched as the applause meter surged from golf clap to the real thing.

Afterwards I hid backstage pretending to fuss with my props. I didn't want to face my parents, who would tell me I had been good while their amused smiles told me otherwise. I was in pantyhose. All the parents would chat with other parents, who would all say how great it had been. I would have to congratulate Lady Macbeth and have my picture taken with Lady Macduff—my *wife*—all of us squirming while the adults suggested we get together and play sometime.

I was too old to play.

I made my escape. The heavy door clicked, erasing the small-talk echoes of the auditorium. I ran down the hallway, my hose sliding on the glossy linoleum. I checked both ways before entering the Living Chemistry classroom. It was dark and silent except for the gurgle of the aquarium. No one could see. I tiptoed to the back of the room, where the rows of tiny, quiet moons gestated on the counter. The growth in my Petri dish was now a long-haired guinea pig smooshed between two clear Frisbees. I put a brown paper towel in my hand to keep from leaving fingerprints. I formed a tiny teardrop of drool, and just when it was about to drop, lifted the lid and gently spat on the fuzz of my genius.

Interview with Kelly Kathleen Ferguson

1. So the half-truth in this essay has to do with the labeling of the Petri dish as "inside desk," a sort of humorous private code for "vagina," which is a secret you keep from your teacher and peers. Is there anything you kept secret from your reader? If so, would you mind sharing now?

As soon as I got home and struggled out of that support hose, I suppressed the memory until it came back one day. Then it became the story I told after a few glasses of wine. Then I felt brave enough to write about it for a workshop. Then I got a good response and felt okay about sending it out to literary magazines. Then it was picked up by *Witness*.

Now that I've told all, maybe the only secret left is that even though I write memoir, I don't enjoy revealing personal stories about myself. But I love stories and feel this need to try and tell interesting stories, and I've learned if characters aren't revealing something about themselves, then what we have is a first semester MFA workshop story that involves a great deal of staring into the middle distance. Of course, the other nonfiction workshop problem can be the melodramatic diary entry, where the reader feels violated by personal information. Maybe the trick is the reluctant reveal; the author tells her story, but only by letting out the rope bit by bit.

2. Humor writing requires exaggeration. But is exaggeration a half-truth? Will you point out a part of this essay that contains exaggeration, and explain the difference between what "really happened" (or how it happened) compared to how you depicted it in the essay?

I'm thinking right now about how Zora Neale Hurston used to travel around the South and hang out on stoops, offering prizes to whoever could tell her the biggest lie. The American tall tale is a great tradition. In this case, I think the writer and the reader both know what's going on, so what's a little fish story among friends?

That being said, my story did "really happen," but it was a long time ago. While I remember the play and remember the Petri dish (and asked my parents for what they could remember), I can't promise that the two events played off one another as neatly as I wrote it. And while my descriptions of the growth imply a sentient life form on the move, maybe there wasn't really a bacteria tornado. And maybe the play wasn't that bad. I do know that for me, back then, as a kid, the growth really seemed the biggest ever, and the play the worst ever, and my parents the cruelest ever, so playing those feelings up helps the story.

3. This essay is layered with secrets about the feminine. Do you think that female writers (and female-identified writers) have a more nuanced sense of the secret? What role does the body play in your writing and writing process?

Here's a secret that I've never told before: when I was a preteen and dying to know *what was up there*, I'd sprawl my legs in front of a white princess mirror with a flashlight and invent yoga positions trying to figure myself out. All boys have to do is look down their pants. It could be that by nature women grow up infused with secrets in that our own bodies are a mystery. I mean, I've spent a certain chunk of my life not knowing if I was pregnant or just bloated. That's a weird way to live.

To answer the second half of the question, I usually don't write about my body at all. I'm way too much of a recovering Catholic for that. For us, the body is a little dried-up wafer that melts on the tongue. Maybe Cheryl Strayed set out on the Pacific Coast Trail with a roll of condoms, but in my memoir, I drove around looking for Laura Ingalls Wilder in a dress zipped up to my neck. Although the dress did lend itself to physical comedy, so I suppose I use my body to that effect. Come to think of it, I did the same with my Macduff "costume" and how my embarrassment over wearing my Dad's shirt as a tunic created acute discomfort.

4. What happened after you spit in the dish, at the end of the essay? Did more stuff grow?

I'm thinking government agents in Hazmat suits were called in, but I'll never know for sure. The *Macbeth* performance was the grand finale and that was that. I was then shipped off to my next summer event, swim team or the YMCA or whatever. Can you believe our Girl Scout camp was called Camp Cherry Austin? And the Boy Scouts went to Camp Horne. I suppose I'm going to have to write about that now.

Dog Psychology

Tina Mitchell

If this ideal unconscious or freedom doesn't exist: simply pretend that it does, use fiction, for the sake of survival, for all of our survival.

　　　　　　　　　　　　　　　　—Kathy Acker, *Empire of the Senseless*

MOM WORE SEQUINED SUNGLASSES WHEN SHE RETRIEVED ME FROM LA Cañada Elementary. She said she had to take Lacy to the vet, and the word "vet" ripped across my back like Velcro. Lacy was my dog, a puppy given to me for my ninth birthday, after Mom convinced me German shepherds were the best breed. I had wanted a toy poodle, but Mom said her mom had a poodle she couldn't stand. "I *hate* poodles," she said. When we agreed on a German shepherd, the kind of dog her dad had, Mom ballooned with delight. "They're the most loyal companions. Like when you're sad, they're sad right along with you."

The concrete curb vanished from the passenger-side mirror as Mom pulled into traffic. "Lacy got a hole in her stomach because she tried to kill herself," she continued. "She jumped off the porch into the bushes. I had to pull a stick out of her little belly, but she only needed a few stitches." Although I was relieved Lacy would be okay, emotions flew like electrons out of me, and I kept watch in the mirror because the objects shifting in Mom's past were always closer than they appeared.

Mom was wild, and she barked. She barked at store clerks and the passengers of cars stopped next to us, at my friends and sometimes their parents. "Rrrrr-ruff. Rrrrr-Ruff ruff." I'd roll my eyes, embarrassed, to which Mom replied, "Oh, come on, Sissy, lighten up. When I was a kid, my dad waved at strangers just so they'd spend the day wondering who the hell was waving at them."

Sometimes Mom didn't bark but told different stories about Grandpa—master narratives that poured from her beer-soaked tongue—stories involving rivers of piss, Elvis Presley, and the Colonel from Kentucky Fried Chicken. One afternoon, years before Lacy, Mom chipped the polish from her toenails and told me Rip Van Winkle was my great-great grandpa. "He didn't really fall asleep for twenty years," she added. "He was just a real bad drunk."

I still believed in Santa Claus at the time, and Mom's maiden name was Van Winkle, so I had no reason to doubt her. When I got older, I believed any story with hiccups because doubting only resulted in stories that bit. Heavy with the aroma of barley malt and yeast, Mom's tales shattered coffee tables and busted a nose. These stories were usually about Grandma, the main source of her anger—the anger that wasn't masked by sequined sunglasses.

After Mom took Lacy to a dog psychologist to sort out her depression, we traveled from Los Angeles to Milford, Kansas, in a motor home to spend Christmas with Mom's parents. During the drive, Lacy ate an entire batch of brownies and puppy-splattered the carpet, causing Mom to threaten to give Lacy to the pound. "I can't take it," she shouted. "I just can't take it anymore!" Even when Lacy was well behaved, Mom complained that Lacy had dandruff and maybe even lice—not fleas but lice!—and we simply couldn't keep her. Even if I had considered Mom's exacerbated anger the result of the impending visit with her parents, I would have still worried Lacy would relapse onto another stick, so I cleaned up all the splatter, and if told to sit, I'd sit.

When we got to Milford, where Grandma baked pies and Grandpa cleaned the shit from his blood with a dialysis machine, Mom beamed about Lacy and told Grandpa that Lacy's dad was in the movies. Taking advantage of Grandpa's presence, I asked, "Does this mean we get to keep her?" Mom gasped and jolted her head as if my question was the yank of her chain. "What, are you crazy or somethin'? Of course we're keeping her. We treat Little Lulu like family."

As a character would in a sitcom, I delivered the punch line: "*That's* what I'm afraid of." Everyone laughed, and my wily older brother who was braver and more bruised than me began singing, "Puppyyyyyy Splaaatter!" And all of us busted a gut.

Afraid to fly, Mom frequently drove between California and Kansas to visit her dying dad. When he slipped into a coma, Mom begged her family to pull the plug. When Grandpa awoke, he said he could hear every Goddamn word and for Christ's sake, don't pull the plug. The last time I saw Grandpa, he wore his service uniform and lay in a casket to rest in peace. After the funeral, Mom commissioned a painting based on a Polaroid of herself and Grandpa sitting on a bench in front of Grandpa's used car lot.

In the painting, Grandpa's thick white hair makes him look like a famous TV detective, but instead of a suit, he wears a white-collared shirt, jeans, and blue suspenders. Mom holds her sequined sunglasses in her right hand. She wears mostly black and enough jewelry that half her forearms are cuffed in silver. Then there is her expression. She smiles, but there is too much light and not enough shadow, and Mom's face looks like a lamp under a black shade of short, permed hair. Her cheeks are white light bulbs. This composition bothered me, and I wondered why the artist hadn't taken different liberties. Why did he exchange Grandpa's car lot for a drab concrete wall? The warm color of the wood bench on which Mom and Grandpa sit clashes with the cool color of concrete and creates a tension like ripped Velcro.

I didn't understand the artist's intent until I walked up the basement stairs one night and caught sight of the painting in my periphery. At a glance, I saw the gray wasn't a wall but a representation of a mirror reflecting a background barely far enough behind Mom and Grandpa to be diffuse. This illusion was so realistic, I turned my head to be sure Mom and Grandpa weren't sitting on a bench in the stairwell. From then on, I sprinted up the stairs in fear of Grandpa's ghost.

When Lacy was a puppy, I saw her sleep while her front paw flexed in intervals like lightning, and I thought she was malfunctioning or possessed. I was afraid like the time I saw Mom's eyes darting like fish beneath the surface of her closed lids. I woke up Lacy as I did Mom. "Lacy. Lacy, wake up!" Unlike Mom, whose eyes opened like a dimmer switch, Lacy whipped her head and rolled onto her stomach as if suddenly jerked back into her body. "You're okay," I gasped. Lacy's alien limb scared me several times before I realized it was a sign of her dreaming, at which point I wondered to what specifically a twitching paw referred and what covered eyes could see.

The year we spent Christmas in Kansas, I walked Lacy and Grandpa's dog, Hans, on a trail near the house. Though there was no snow, I wore moon boots because the deep freeze chilled sound waves and shivered in my bones. Unleashed, the dogs were arrows darting up the trail and into a thicket of trees. I bounded after them. I took giant leaps. The rubber platform heels lightened me up up up until I found the dogs dashing across a frozen pond. My stomach sank. Terrified they'd break the surface and drown in translations of chipped nail polish and vet visits, I called for them, but they kept running. Hans's tan shoulders and haunches stretched like a wolf's while Lacy, a shadow of fur, chased after him. Verging on panic, I called again. My voice ricocheted off the slab of ice. I yelled again and again. Then I remembered a science lesson: Dog paws are wired with ultrasonic transducers that can test the thickness and density of ice. If the ice is too thin, an alarm will sound and they'll back off, which is why northerners use sled dogs to traverse glaciers. Only partially convinced this lesson was fact, I kept an eye on the dogs as long as possible by walking backwards to the trail. When the dogs finally saw me leaving, they followed me home.

Mom was wearing pajamas and watching TV when I came home from school and noticed the empty space where the painting had hung for nearly a decade. Acetone-soaked cotton balls smeared with dark enamel were piled on the coffee table in front of her, and she was preparing to polish her nails light blue. "Why'd you take down the painting of Grandpa?" I asked.

"Because I'm mad at him," she said. I knew she resented him for drinking and staying married to my abusive grandma, but this was the first time she said so without embellishing the truth with a hilarious story, so I asked why, and she barked. "He's long dead and gone. It doesn't matter." I was in high school and wouldn't resolve to bite back for another decade, so I let lying dogs sleep and went to my room, where the cold mattered, like an electric current under my skin.

Lacy's bones shrank under her skin, and by the time I was in college, she'd get disoriented and walk into walls. When her hip dysplasia put her in chronic pain, Mom had her put to sleep. Her death dissolved part of me into atmosphere, and when I think about her now, I feel absence like a hole and the gravity of nothing. I'll never get another dog.

Mom has since had more than a handful of dogs. Betsy and Neiman were her favorites. Betsy was a German shepherd. Neiman, a Jack Russell terrier. Neiman barked at mirrors, flashlights, and ceilings as if he, like me, saw Grandpa's ghost. "Betsy and Neiman are my beacons of light and love in this world of darkness and cruelty," Mom would say. She commissioned their portrait. The dogs are shown sitting in the living room, and the background is detailed all the way down to the red plaid fabric of the ottoman. The painting hangs in place of Mom and Grandpa's, which is kept in the concrete safe room in the basement.

Mom smothers her new dog with kisses. Elly Mae is a cairn terrier. "Like Toto," Mom says. "And she is really protective of me, so don't get too close or she'll bite." When it's time for me to leave, Mom and Elly follow me to the door, and Mom jokes, "Come on now and give Mummy a hug." I tell her nice try, and we both laugh at the punch line barking between us.

Interview with Tina Mitchell

1. There is a tricky knot between family lies, family secrets, and family compassion—when we know something to be true, but we keep it in the subtext out of empathy. This unusual essay doesn't fully reveal exactly what's going on, but it's there in the subtext. What do you want beginning writers to learn from this style?

I'm not sure I can add much to the conversation on subtext, so I refer writers to Hemingway, the father of the iceberg theory, and Charles Baxter's *The Art of Subtext: Beyond Plot*. It's my suspicion that subtext, enormously complicated, is also rather intuitive. We are well-adapted creatures in part because we learn to avoid pain, so if we must confront a painful situation, our instincts tell us to do so in the way that causes the least amount of pain. For me, that meant relying on subtext to turn a dramatic story into what I hope is kind of a funny one. The tricky part about relying on subtext in nonfiction is learning to see your blind spots. A writer must overcome her instincts in order to know exactly what she's deflecting; otherwise it's likely the story won't ring true.

2. How did you settle on the title? Some of the essays in this anthology have in their titles obvious references to secrets and half-truths; yours does not. Or does it?

While the title is a direct reference to the trip my mom and Lacy took to a dog psychologist (who said we weren't to call Lacy "lop-eared dog" because it hurt her feelings), the title also refers to the subconscious and the symbolic, in addition to a kind of "kick-the-dog syndrome," when anger is displaced on an innocent person or pet. I also hoped the title would resonate with Pavlov's dogs and classical and operant conditioning. Behaviorism is a learning method but also a means of control. No secrets here but the truth below the surface.

3. Where some readers will want a more direct reflection of the secrets in this family, other readers will notice that this essay captures how hard it is to write about family secrets. Who are some of your influences for this style of writing?

To be honest, I hardly ever read narrative memoirs about families. I read Annie Dillard religiously and love a good lyric essay. I was recently inspired by Dawn S. Davies's "Disquiet and the Lyric Essay." In the opening, she writes, "Deborah Tall and John D'Agata say that 'the lyric essay does not expound, that it may merely mention,' which causes Gen Xers and ADDers like me to be like, phew, that's a relief, because screw it, I can't write any other way." Other than that, my work is influenced by a hodgepodge of literature and theory from the nineteenth to twenty-first centuries.

Invisible Nails

Samuel Autman

I CURLED ON THE FLOOR BETWEEN TWO PEWS, MY HANDS COVERING MY FACE. I screamed and sobbed like never before, the yell of someone losing a limb to an axe or saw, a gut-busting shriek that poured from my innermost being. Wrath and a specific Christian shame moved through my vocal chords, as if something in me, but not of me, was crying through me. Sorrow and embarrassment became a braid of tears and mucous on my chin. I felt so spiritually and physically exposed I might as well be masturbating in front of my mother while standing on a stage under a spotlight. My six-foot-four 220-pound worked-out frame stood out as one of a dozen black bodies in a sea of eight hundred mostly white and female attendees. A soft, warm feminine hand touched my shoulders, a needed physical reassurance. "You're gonna be all right, brother. It's okay." I recognized the voice as my friend Jenny. From the back of the auditorium, Erma's "Glory to God!" and "Hallelujahs!" reverberated, ever Jesus's cheerleader. I had come because Erma had convinced me it was God's will. A male usher grabbed my right arm and then hand as I struggled to my feet. I shook off the embarrassment and sat back in the pew. Besides, it wasn't my fault. If John fell out as if into a deep sleep at Jesus's feet in the Book of Revelation, how was I supposed to respond? When the power hits, you fall, no matter how ridiculous you look. I wasn't going to reveal how embarrassed I was by the incident. That's the way Pentecostals do it. Whether it's cavorting or falling out, they have their minute-and-a-half performance before the congregation. It ends. They return to their seat as if nothing has happened.

The collapse took place near the front of the Edman Memorial Chapel in Wheaton, Illinois, at a conference called Pastoral Care Ministries in the summer of 2002. I don't fully understand what happened. I still don't. All I know is when the fragile Leanne Payne stood behind a wooden lectern, she triggered me like no other preacher. The whole episode caught me off-guard. I had been in Pentecostal church services off and on all my life. Why was this different?

With her big glasses, dimpled grin, and gray hair pulled back in a bun, she resembled a character on an oatmeal canister, a marketer's dream of a sweet grandmother. The microphone transformed that warm, soft voice into a thunderous, hypnotic shrill. Oh, how her frequency short-circuited my own spiritual radio station. The jitters in my stomach afterward made me want to vomit in between the pews, where, just moments before, I had lain hollering as if out of my mind. I didn't. Life's most upside-down moment, a black man in a room filled with white women, a gay man who sought to be heterosexual. Months prior to that moment, I wore a purple Polynesian wrap and stood on the sidelines cheering in San Diego's gay pride parade, such contrast to encrusted guilt and shame. When they commingled they left a stain like tar, not easily washed away.

For the last few years I had been inhaling Payne's tapes and books, *Crisis in Masculinity* and *The Broken Image: Restoring Personal Wholeness through Healing Prayer*, staples of ex-gay ministries worldwide, at Erma's beckoning. At forty-five years old, she radiated a toothy smile, big hair, and a kindness I found irresistible. I had known Erma since I was a fifteen-year-old boy sitting on homosexual tendencies he hadn't acted on yet. Although there were years we were out of touch when I "backslid," Erma's comforting "Hallelujah brother" was always a phone call away. My prayer partner for years, she'd determined that through this ministry, an affiliate of Exodus International, she believed she had found a way to pray me out of being gay. My attachment to Erma bordered on codependence at least, spiritual Stockholm syndrome at worst. Her kindness and our common history in the Church of God in Christ, a black Pentecostal church, bound us. Over the years she managed to worm her way into my skull. When I listened, she decreed where I didn't stick my dick.

Months prior to the Wheaton incident, I lay prostrate on a carpet in my San Diego apartment sobbing as the World Trade towers collapsed on my TV screen. God was a box I disappeared into every few years. The voice from the box beckoned, filled me with shame, declared my homosexuality as wicked, defiled, and ungodly, yet I returned to the box.

Chris, the blond man who led the prayer, laid his hand palm down on my scalp. He resembled Mormon missionaries I saw on the streets when I lived in Salt Lake City: clean-cut, early twenties, and skinny. I sat in the circle surrounded by other "homosexual strugglers" who with closed eyes and bowed heads in Grace Chapel Church's basement in San Diego focused their attention for a few minutes. They knew I had been hooking up with a buddy for sex in my North Park apartment just a few blocks away. They prayed anyway.

"Dear Lord Jesus, please help my brother Samuel overcome these same-sex attraction issues." The joint pressure from their collective hands made my head sweat. "Lord, you know his heart's desire is to follow you and do the right thing. Jesus help him be the man you want him to be. In your name we pray. Amen."

No one raised his voice. Nor did their bodies jerk with God's electrical surge I associated with Pentecostal prayer. Everyone present spoke in a whisper, a deep awe. Afterward they mashed a crucifix on my head and poured on holy water, drenching my shirt. The water had been blessed beforehand, just as Leanne Payne outlined in *The Broken Image: Restoring Personal Wholeness through Healing Prayer.* According to Payne's philosophy, Christians needed symbols to release faith. God didn't need those trinkets, but humans did to manifest His invisible kingdom in the physical. The men seated in the room had come from throughout San Diego County and paid hundreds of dollars to participate in "Living Waters: Pursuing Sexual and Relational Wholeness in Christ," a six-month course that mixed Christianity and counseling, to reorient us to heterosexuality. Desert Stream Ministries, located ninety miles north in Anaheim, wrote the manual and trained the ministers. They were convinced heartfelt prayer aligned with the manual could eradicate "homosexual tendencies."

The manual's chapters included such titles as "The Father's Pursuit of Us," "Welcoming Him into Our Brokenness," and "The Cross: Resurrecting the True Self," mixed heavy doses of Christian therapy with Vineyard Ministries style. They were a worldwide charismatic denomination, which like other Pentecostals emphasized the gifts and manifestations of the Holy Spirit, loud music, speaking in tongues, prophecy, healing, and the casting out of demons. The congregants were mostly middle- and upper-middle-class whites with a few blacks, Asians, and Latinos. Their preachers wore more tie-dye than suits and ties. The San

Diego Vineyard was so progressive it held Sunday services at a bar in Pacific Beach, such a contrast to the judgmental God of my youth.

The men in the basement that day at Grace Church believed homosexuality was unnatural, foul, and an abomination before a holy God. Thus, the gay self needed not just rehabilitation but crucifixion with prayer, fasting, and many hours lying on the floor, prostrate. Their faith departed from curing or makeover. The gay self needed to be excised until a new self arose. Jesus, through their prayers, was calling forth the true me, the Lazarus in a tomb. All of that "lifestyle" hooking up, masturbating, drinking, and going to the gay bars were grave clothes covering the true me. They wanted to end my fun.

I wanted to believe that the true me was a Christian self that had not been awakened to God. In order for that self to come forth, I needed to help kill this funner me. I wasn't sure that was possible, but if the Scriptures were true and God raised Jesus from the dead, and Jesus opened blind eyes and cleansed the lepers, couldn't that same resurrection power zap me into heterosexuality? Either it worked or it didn't. We all hugged each other as we said our goodbyes—key because part of "gender neurosis" was rooted in "unhealthy boundaries with men." I did wonder how big a few of their dicks were, especially one guy who always leaned back in his chair and did the man spread.

I hopped in my car, tossed the *Living Waters Manual* on the back seat, and went home. Within minutes, I logged onto my AOL's gay chat room. *Why am I doing this? Ten minutes ago, was I not sitting in a room full of Christian men trying to feel the power and get free?* One of my AOL buddies instant-messaged me:

"Hey Sam? Where you been?"

"Oh, here and there, working a lot."

"We need to connect man. It's been a long time since I rode that dick."

"Sounds good man. I'm tired. Long day and I gotta be at work early. We'll connect soon."

"Man, did I do something to piss you off? You've been pretty distant lately."

"LOL. It's not you. Just me and my shit. Under a lot of pressure. We'll get together soon. Ciao."

"Bye stud."

My body shook. Tim was a masculine hair stylist at a high-end salon who loved getting brunch on Sundays, either at Café on Park or Hash House A Go Go in Hillcrest, the gay neighborhood. We went nude bathing at Black's Beach in La Jolla, strolling past the straight people for the furthest end of the beach—the gay section. Guys there couldn't wait to drop their Speedos, lounge naked on towels, and smear sunblock on one another's backs. Sometimes men sucked each other off or actually fucked—way outside my personal comfort zone, but I admired their sheer boldness. It felt right. Although Tim lived less than a mile away from me, and I craved to see him, I didn't. I knew where it would lead. Ours was what I saw among legions of gay men in those days—not quite boyfriends but more than fuck buddies.

I snapped out of it and called Erma, the most Christian woman I knew.

"I just got back from Living Waters. It's going okay. We're in a really hard part."

"Don't let the enemy trick you, brother. We'll be going to see Leanne in a few months. Now she has power with God. I've never seen anything like it, Samuel. You talking about someone who's walking the walk. This woman is on a whole other level. Her walk with God is awesome. You'll really connect with her."

As she spoke of Leanne Payne, a certain hope arose within me. Like Jesus and the woman with the issue of blood, she said to herself, "If I just touch the hem of his garment, I know I will be made whole." If I could just get to this Leanne Payne conference and have her pray with me, I knew I would be made straight. Erma prayed for me and we got off the phone. Maybe this Leanne Payne, who Erma had been talking about for more than a year, held the answers to my twenty years of seesawing in and out of church.

The day before my spiritual nervous breakdown in front of the other conference attendees at the Edman Chapel, I stood in the doorway of the Wheaton College main dining hall looking at the rainfall. It wasn't a calm Midwestern drizzle, but rather the torrential Arkansas downpours I had seen as a child. I knew I'd never see a harder water pressure fall from the sky. Inside my heart I heard, "Let it rain, let it rain. Open the floodgates of Heaven," from Michael W. Smith's live CD *Worship*. I cried. My soul opened, that sweet feeling of expansion and splendor that happened when I walked my bedroom floor with my hands lifted. In moments like those I knew true unity, oneness with the Creator, and creation crafted just for me. The madness that compelled me to seek heterosexuality melted in those splendid seconds. The lyrics looped inside. Marvelous "all is well" moments made the struggle worthwhile. I knew if The Lamb's Book of Life opened, I'd see *Samuel Anthony Autman Jr.* inscribed therein. Total, perfect love—no judgment or condemnation or people imposing their version of God. The softness of God arose within. These moments were rarely shared with a group and were musically induced. God felt deeply personal and on my side.

Payne looked resplendent in her white, flowing Episcopal vestments as she marched down the aisle in a processional with her ministry team. The accoutrements reminded me of things I had seen in Catholic churches. The caravan carried a large metal crucifix, burning incense, and holy water. Pipe organs blared. Payne loved rituals, symbols, and images that she feared Christianity had turned away from since Martin Luther and the Reformation. In her books, Payne flailed against Protestants who had "foolishly smashed the idols" used by the Roman Catholic Church. By doing so, she said, they lost a vital link to the divine. The Edman Chapel on Wheaton College's campus had a fire-truck-red carpet, tan wooden pews, and stained-glass windows depicting scenes from the Four Gospels, all congruent with Payne's costume. Having grown up in the black Protestant churches, the highness and formality of ceremony left me awed. I'm definitely from a "low."

When she arrived at the lectern, Payne bowed her head and gave a long invocation. She looked up, relying heavily on lecture notes and Bible verses that she had been using for years. For forty-five minutes she argued that Americans, even in the church world, worshipped at the altars of Baal and Ashtoreth more than Jesus.

"If you are returning to the Lord with all your hearts then rid yourself of the foreign gods and the Astoreths and commit yourself to the Lord and serve him only!" she said, quoting 1 Samuel 7:3–4. "And He will deliver you out of the hand of the Philistines. So the Israelites put away their Baals and Ashtoreths and served the Lord only."

Payne loved talking about the "sin of misogyny" or the hatred of women, which, she asserted, went hand in hand with the modern worship of Baal. Pointing to passages from German Canadian psychiatrist and philosopher Karl Stern's book *The Flight from Woman*, she said that society's and the church's suppression of women had stifled the expression of God's feminine aspects and overemphasized the paternal—a not-subtle jab at the papacy. She pushed her glasses up, looked at the crowd periodically, and went back to her notes like the college professor she had been for decades.

"This was the vice underlying the homosexuality found in Greece during the classic times," she said. Because of it, women were not considered a fit companion for men, which led to homosexuality and ultimately Rome's fall. I didn't understand the link or her thinking, but the numerous theologians she quoted gave her an air of authority. Payne was just getting fired up.

"Due to the grossly sexual nature of Baal worship, most of the Bible commentators leave out the details on the kinds of orgies that its worship leads to."

According to Payne's interpretation of the Bible, the Children of Israel had periodically taken to worshipping Baal and Ashtoreth, the gods of the Phoenicians. Ashtoreth is cited as the queen of heaven. Payne called her Baal's wife and female counterpart.

"I don't even like to talk about this," Payne said. She then referenced "lascivious lifestyle," "lewd practices," "perversion," and "licentious behavior." "It's the worship of one's own procreative faculties, phallic demons." In other words, they were demons that looked like penises.

My stomach muscles tightened as she spoke. Her presence in the regalia, her scholarship and presentation were formidable. She was no slouch. It didn't matter to me. Something in me revolted against her words. If I were to follow her philosophy, I would have had to stop watching Showtime's *Queer as Folk*. The Brian character would have definitely worshiped penises in those bathhouse orgy scenes. For me, this would mean no more trips to Black's Beach with Tim, or three-day getaways to the clothing-optional hotel in Palm Springs. Payne wanted to rip all of the fun out of my life and banish me to a life conforming to her boring doctrines. No more gay male magazines with sculpted bodies and go-go boys dancing on the bars. I was beginning to feel like a dick worshipper and the condemnation felt dreadful. Every word Payne spoke drove a dagger into me—the hard words from a woman who appeared sweet. Beneath that robe she had invisible nails in her hands and they delivered death blows to my gay self—a gay self I had abandoned and reconstructed and abandoned again.

"How long will you waiver between two opinions? If the Lord is God, follow him; if Baal, follow him."

The deities and practices must be not only repented for, but also verbally confessed and renounced by name, she said. "Ministry team, get the holy water." She ordered the team's men to step back, because exposing the sin of misogyny sometimes caused women to react negatively to men. Her voice now roared its hypnotic chant/yell in the way that only old-fashioned Pentecostals do. The row of white women in front of me, the woman next to me in a pantsuit, and a handsome man three seats down in jeans hugged their Bibles. They were all—and I repeated her words too—declarations of liberty from Old Testament deities. Payne's view was clear: These were wicked spirits in high places.

I renounce you Baal.

I renounce you Baal.

I renounce you Ashtoreth.

I renounce you Ashtoreth.

I renounce you in the name of Jesus.

I renounce you in the name of Jesus.

I renounce the sin of misogyny.

I renounce the sin of misogyny.

I renounce the idol gods my fathers served.

I renounce the idol gods my fathers served.

Somewhere along the prayer, I stopped repeating after Payne and started to scream. "Noooooooooooooooo!" Embarrassment—and in no small part, my Pentecostal training—kicked in, and I fell to the floor, sobbing.

"See, there it is, right there." I imagined the minister pointing at my heaving frame. "I command any unclean spirits to manifest at this time. If there's any manifestation, look up and see how the Lord will destroy that. In the name of the Father and of the Son and of the Holy Spirit. May this put you in remembrance of your baptism!"

I erupted in pain, anger, and revulsion. Spiritually, I vomited every word back in shrieks and yells. I couldn't stop. Payne called it a demonic manifestation. I called it pain. As other people began to scream, some convulsed and fell too; ushers scuttled about the altar assisting them.

Payne began expressing glossolalia, speaking in the longest, most complicated syllables in tongues, sounding almost Germanic. Not like the "ah bah, bah, bah" or "he coming on a Honda" kind of stuff I had heard in some churches. While I sobbed, memories flashed through my head.

I cried for my sister Syrethia back in St. Louis, who lived in a group home with a kind of schizophrenia, which forced her to regularly run nude through her living quarters, assaulting employees and knocking over furniture. When she terrorized me and my mother with this behavior, I didn't flinch at dragging her before the congregation to have a preacher attempt to drive spirits from her. In that moment I was as the Gadarene demoniac, one who according to Scripture was so demon-possessed he lived among the tombs, and screamed and flailed at the sight and words of Jesus. I owed my sister an apology.

I cried for Samuel Anthony Autman Sr., my absentee father who seven years prior died face-down in the dirt, like a dog, frozen to death outside, clutching two 40-ounce bottles of beer. The vacant lot where he died was a mere two hours and forty minutes from Wheaton in Peoria, Illinois. His life and absence seeded my lifelong spiritual journey.

I cried for the monumental disappointment that was the *San Diego Union-Tribune*, a newspaper that promised inclusiveness in its hiring and coverage, but couldn't shake its right-leaning tendencies. For the last six months my gut had been screaming to leave. For thirteen years I had labored as a reporter at papers including the *Tulsa World*, the *Salt Lake Tribune*, and the *St. Louis Post-Dispatch*, and had both loved and hated print journalism. Had I pissed away a promising career and jeopardized my livelihood on a crazy, religious whim? With no job prospects, and only one book idea, I was more vulnerable than hopeful. If all else failed, I hoped I could crawl back to daily newspapers.

In the depth of my despair, I felt a hand pat me on the shoulders, and a voice whispered into my ear. "It's gonna be all right. Just go ahead and cry and let it all out." I looked up and saw Jenny, my other friend who had come to this conference with me from the San Diego Vineyard. She had sat a few rows in front of me. Her face mixed pity, pained relief, and painful glee. I cringed. Jenny knew the drill. Erma's "Glory to God!" and "Thank you Jesus!" rang from the back of the sanctuary, distinctive and irritating. Erma loved that I had fallen out in front of these people. She said I had been too dignified. In her mind, my collapse proved Payne's prayers and conference had worked. My foul gay demons had been cast into outer darkness.

When the service ended, my being felt as light as it had in years. I composed myself, walked to the back of the sanctuary, and perused the books on the table. Before long, Erma, Jenny, and I convened in the church's orange brick courtyard. Dazed under June's hot sun, I chitchatted, embarrassed and confused, while they feigned conversation. The women hadn't been getting along, and we lapsed into awkward silence.

"Well, brother, obviously you lost a few devils," Erma said, placing her hand over her mouth and chuckling in a loud country way. Mississippi leaked through.

"I guess so, huh?"

"Samuel, that was amazing. I think God totally delivered you from the lifestyle," Jenny said. "It was so gnarly."

I didn't know what the word gnarly meant, but my white friends used it all the time.

I knew screaming was good for the soul and I had a lot to release.

On the way back to my dorm room, I stopped at a bench and called Steve, a guy I had found through the Internet. He was a tall, lean brunet to whom I was very attracted, and he had planned to relocate from Los Angeles to San Diego. The plan was he'd move in with me to save money. With no income, a roommate would offset my Southern California lifestyle while I searched for another job.

"Hi, Steve."

"Hey man. What's going on? How's Chicago?"

"It's okay. I need to tell you something." I paused. "I've decided I no longer want a roommate. I'm gonna keep living by myself for a while."

Silence. Then, "Why? What's happened?"

The roots of Baal worship had been blasted out of my being that day, I wanted to say. I had convinced myself. I wasn't turning back. Jesus would forgive me for not being completely forthcoming. It was a lie by omission, but why cast my pearls before swine? I knew that had Steve become my roommate, I might have acted out. I wanted to shut the door to Baal.

"It's not you. I just decided I want to keep living alone and thought it would be best to tell you before you moved all the way from L.A. Sorry, man."

"I guess. Well, okay."

I hung up—sure I had done God's will. Issues of keeping my word and pulling the rug out from under someone didn't occur to me. I just wanted to get right with God. Many temptations lay before me in San Diego—all those muscle boys. The last thing I needed was a man I found attractive walking around my condo in boxers and a tank top.

Several days later in San Diego, Jenny and her friend Jodie came to my condo to help me cleanse the place of the ungodly books I had accumulated. In the Acts, when the Christians were delivered from wickedness, the apostles ordered them to burn their curious arts and books. I felt uneasy about parting with books, but I wanted to follow God.

Jenny and Jodie began boxing up any book that didn't have the word Bible, Jesus, or church in the title. *Talking at the Gates: A Life of James Baldwin*, by James

Campbell, ended up in the pile, as did Maya Angelou's *Wouldn't Take Nothing for My Journey*, and *Beefcake: The Muscle Magazines of America 1950–1970*.

"What about this one? This one doesn't feel good to me either, brother. It's gotta go," Jodie said. They never added any book to the stack that I didn't nod my agreement to, but I felt double-minded. In the service of God's kingdom and in pursuit of heterosexuality, I conceded.

"We'll take these away for you," Jodie said, clutching a stack of books.

"Oh, don't worry about it. I'll take them to the Goodwill or something."

"Are you sure? We're happy to take them," Jenny said.

I assured them I'd handle them. After they left, I put the book crates in my two-car garage. Surely God would help me want to throw away books that were leading me astray. Maybe the desire would come. But soon, I decided to keep the books. They were mine. Would I want to worship a God who opposed intellectual expression? A few weeks later, I heard Oprah Winfrey talk about how Eckhart Tolle's *The Power of Now* had changed her life. I bought it in hardback. As I read it, something broke wide open. I read about the concept of the "pain-body," an accumulation of one's unconscious emotional pains. The author likens the pain-body to an energetic entity. Once confronted, some people cried out like the demons described in the New Testament. The insight made me smile. A feeling of inner vastness unlike anything I've ever experienced—so deep, so wide, and so peaceful—unfolded within me. So splendid, regal, royal, majestic—a sweet, wonderful feeling enveloped me each time I read the passages.

A print called *The Moorish Chief* hung in my living room. I had purchased it at the Philadelphia Museum of Art in the late 1990s. The picture spoke to me on a spiritual and physical level because the image focused on a handsome, muscular, dark-skinned man who was aristocratic. A tall man in a long, flowing white robe, he stood in the doorway of a palace. No one knew if he was a real person in his environment or an artist's model. He looked like a god who had fallen from the sky, humanity and divinity in the face of a black man. His physical demeanor signified dominion.

Over the next few years, I learned to sit in the silence until that sweet, peaceful feeling arose from within, the same sensation I had felt when I saw the rainfall and heard Michael W. Smith's song that day in Wheaton. Sometimes the feeling came over me in the shower, or while driving and certain songs came on—it could be Donna Summer's "On the Radio," or any tune that tapped life's sweet frequency. It's a frequency of love, joy, and extreme peace. It's a vibration of ultimate well-being. I still love the Scriptures, and through meditation I move into that blissful interior palace where all that I am is loved, nurtured, and embraced. I recognize that Erma and Jenny were friendly people who helped orchestrate the near-crucifixion of my true self with the nails of their friendship. Erma and I remained in contact. The last time she prayed for me on the phone she said she felt some kind of a barrier.

"What was that?"

I was silent. Listening. I was not screaming, not shouting "Noooooo!" In the silence I was removing the nails I couldn't see and dancing to the rhythm of the song emanating from my own soul.

Interview with Samuel Autman

1. What motivated you to write this and publish this, in essence to share this time in your life with an audience of strangers? (or, perhaps, the audience isn't strangers?) Have you received any comments from readers? Has Erma or Jenny read the piece?

When I was enrolled in Columbia University's MFA program, I got the idea while taking Phillip Lopate's survey class "The Art of the Personal Essay," named for the anthology he had compiled. We studied Montaigne, Plutarch, and numerous contemporary essayists. Although it was not a workshop, he was kind enough to read and critique an early draft then called "The Boys of Baal." His generosity and kind words gave me confidence to submit it in a workshop at Columbia, where they eviscerated it, but because Professor Lopate liked it, I knew I had something. I've been rewriting and submitting the piece to contests and literary magazines for the last decade. The piece's evolution reflected my own. Along the way I got encouraging personal rejection notes from editors, including a really nice note from John D'Agata. With Lopate and D'Agata's words behind me, I kept rewriting it until I got it right. The piece landed me a New York City literary agent's confidence and became the seed of my manuscript *Sanctified: A Memoir*, which covers the same issues but goes back to my childhood. Winning the SLS-Disquiet International nonfiction prize and seeing it published in the

Ninth Letter's website thrilled me. I know the audience for literary magazines is highly select. If Erma has read it, and we are still in contact, she hasn't mentioned it. I've lost contact with Jenny.

2. There are some amazing, show-stopping metaphors in this essay, which reminds us that it's not enough to just write up the shocking details of a secret—authors need to aim for artistic style and precision as well (which is a different kind of "shock.") What is your process for writing lines like "God was a box I disappeared into every few years"? Why not "God was like a box I disappeared into every few years" or "I became very religious every few years"?

Thank you. The phrase "God was a box I disappeared into every few years" came from free writing sessions quite early in the process. That helps me generate raw memories and feelings that I plug into the work. The other phrases you referenced—Why not "God was like a box I disappeared into every few years" or "I became very religious every few years"?—aren't as fresh, nor do they capture the guttural feeling I hoped to evoke. I believe poetic imagery sharpens the personal essay. Over the years my concept of an angry Old Testament God has imploded, which I really wanted to underscore.

3. It's interesting that you were a journalist before switching to creative writing. Will you explain some of differences between how a reporter has to handle a cover-up (for example, a local politician gets caught in a complex lie or subterfuge) compared to how a creative nonfiction writer can handle secrets?

A local politician has hurled him or herself into the public arena. In the United States privacy is a thing of the past, especially for elected officials. Politicians are often elected or appointed. With that comes a massive invasion of privacy. That's just given. The bigger the politician, the less mercy reporters and bloggers will have. That's just part of the game. They know that when they get involved. In this essay I used pseudonyms for the people who are still living, if they might come across in a less than flattering light. That's what I did for Erma and Jenny. Leanne Payne, who is now dead, had authored several books. It just so happens that in the larger work, the people who might not come across so well—my father, a few ministers, and both of my grandmothers—are deceased. I'll name them. Pseudonyms aren't encouraged in the journalism I grew up reading and writing. The rules are different in nonfiction. Their stories matter more than their real names.

4. Who have you read, perhaps as a "literary mentor," that helped you decide how, or why, to write this essay?

James Baldwin's *Notes on a Native Son* for his courage and embedded biblical references. Dinty W. Moore's *Between Panic and Desire* because it's an unconventional memoir arguably threaded together by personal essays. Also, he had been a print journalist who made the leap so he's a special writer to me. I loved Kathleen Harrison's *The Kiss* and Alice Sebold's *Lucky* for their boldness. These are texts that impacted me a lot.

White Lies

Erin Murphy

ARPI, A LEBANESE GIRL WHO PRONOUNCED *ASK* AS *AX* NO MATTER HOW MANY times the teacher corrected her, must have been delighted by the arrival of Connie, the new girl in our fifth grade class. Connie was albino, exceptionally white even by the ultra-Caucasian standards of our southern suburb. Only her eyelids had color: mouse-nose pink, framed by moth-white lashes and brows.

We had been taught that there was no comparative or superlative for *different*. Things were either different or the same, the teacher said. Likewise for *perfect*—something was either perfect or not. But surely Arpi thought of Connie as *more different* than herself. Arpi may have had a name that sounded all too close to Alpo, a brand of dog food, but at least she had a family whose skin and hair and eyes looked like hers. Connie, by comparison, was alone in her difference. She was, perhaps, *most different. Differentest.*

This was confirmed by the ridicule, which was immediate and unrelenting: *Casper, Chalk Face, Q-Tip.* Connie, whose shoulders hunched in a permanent parenthesis, pretended not to hear the names or the taunting questions: *What'd ya do, take a bath in bleach? Who's your boyfriend—Frosty the Snowman?* She sat

---

Names have been changed to protect privacy.

in the front of the classroom, and if she felt the boys plucking white hairs from her scalp, she didn't react. The teacher, who was serving the last nine months of a thirty-year sentence in the public school system, spent the bulk of each day perusing magazines and L.L. Bean catalogs in the back of the room. As far as I know, she never intervened.

All of this changed in mid-October when Connie's father got a job at a candy factory, news Connie announced tentatively one rainy day during indoor recess.

Can he get us candy?

Yes.

Any kind? As much as we want? For free?

Yes, yes, yes.

And so the daily ritual began. Kids placed orders for Reese's Cups, Baby Ruth bars, Hubba Bubba bubble gum. Connie kept a log of the requests in a pocket-sized notebook. The next day, she would tote a box full of candy into the classroom and distribute the promised sweets to eager hands. Overnight, Connie became the center of attention. Girls—even Marcia Miller, the first in our class to wear mascara—would beg to sit by Connie at lunch so they could update their orders.

And what about me? What was my role? Did I request my favorites—Three Musketeers and coconut-centered Mounds bars? Or did I, as I have told myself and others in the years since, refuse to contribute to such cruelty? Or, in a more likely scenario, did I dump out my loot triumphantly at home one afternoon, only to be scolded by my mother? I don't remember—my memory obscured, I'm sure, by the wishful image of myself as a precocious champion of social justice. And I don't remember if I actually witnessed—or just imagined—Connie and her mother at the 7-Eleven one day after school. They were in the candy aisle. Her mother was filling a cardboard box. And Connie, bathed in unflinching fluorescence, was curved over her notebook making small, careful check marks.

Interview with Erin Murphy

1. This essay is layered with elementary school secrets. For example, the phrase "even Marcia Miller, the first in our class to wear mascara" speaks of a secret knowledge among girls. What advice do you have for writers who want to plumb their school day secrets for essays? Which ones are right to share, and how do you know?

Secrets beget secrets. For every one you remember, there are others lurking. The Marcia reference, for example, has a larger backstory. She started wearing mascara and blue eye shadow, probably not even that much by today's standards. Her mother didn't approve, so Marcia would apply it on the bus in the morning and wipe it off on the ride home. For some reason, I had very strong feelings about this. I remember passing a note to her that said, "You don't need makeup to be beautiful." I cringe when I think of this. Yet it was, I think, the first rumblings of feminism brewing in my ten-year-old body. It may be worth noting that nearly forty years later, I still don't wear makeup, though I've stopped judging women who do. That story got pared down to one sentence in this essay, but it could easily become an essay of its own. The trick, I think, is to find where you fit into the story. If you're just spilling someone else's secrets, your work probably won't rise above gossip. But if you can reflect on how the untold story relates to you or to something larger, you may be able to spin the secret into art.

2. Most of the essays in this anthology are long, because some secrets take a lot of explaining. So why did you choose the brief essay or "flash nonfiction" format? What other writers do this?

There is what's said in the essay, and there is what's mostly unsaid: that for my entire adult life I've crafted the narrative of myself as a longtime champion of social justice. Some of this is based on empirical facts, such as the story my mother tells of the day I came home crying because a boy in third grade hadn't received any Valentine's cards. But certainly there were times when I could be as shallow as the meanest of the 'tween girls. The story of Connie gave me the opportunity to examine one particular instance in which I might not have been as enlightened as I'd like to think I was. That's the real secret—or lie—of the essay, and yet it exists in the conditional, what Lisa Knopp aptly calls "perhapsing."

Judith Kitchen edited several excellent anthologies of brief nonfiction (*In Short, Short Takes, In Brief*), and Dinty W. Moore has showcased the finest contemporary creative nonfiction essays of 750 words or fewer in his online journal *Brevity*. In most of these essays, the "unsaid" would, if written, increase the length of the pieces exponentially.

3. At the end, you wonder what your role was, and you question a key part of your memory (and the secret). Was that a way to protect Connie's privacy,

even after so many years? When writers are revealing someone else's secret, what are some general ethical guidelines to follow?

I questioned my memory not to protect anyone but to expose myself. This is a story I had told one way over the years, but when I sat down to write the essay, I realized I may not have been as blameless as I had given myself credit for being. In terms of protecting the privacy of Connie and the others, I changed the names. That's one option open to writers. Some nonfiction writers also create composite characters that would be difficult to trace to real people; while I did not do this in "White Lies," I can appreciate how it may be the most ethical—and certainly the most efficient—way to protect identities and highlight a particular memory. In this case, however, I think it's important to note this in the preface or in the piece itself. After all, the most pressing ethical guideline we face as creative nonfiction writers is to tell the truth.

Reading History to My Mother

Robin Hemley

Your silence will not protect you.

—Audre Lourde

"Everything's mixed up in those boxes, the past and the present," my mother tells me. "Those movers made a mess of everything." I'm visiting her at the Leopold late on a Monday night after reading to my kids and being read to by my eldest, Olivia, who at six is rightfully proud of her newfound reading ability. My mother and I have been readers for many years, but in some ways, she finds reading more difficult than does Olivia. At eighty-two, my mother's eyesight has deteriorated. Glaucoma. Severe optic nerve damage to her left eye. Macular degeneration. Tomorrow, I'm taking her to the doctor for a second laser operation to "relieve the pressure." We have been told by the doctor that the surgery won't actually improve her eyesight, but, with luck, will stop it from deteriorating any more. After that there's another operation she'll probably undergo, eighty miles south in Seattle. Another operation that won't actually make her see any better.

"I always had such good eyesight," she tells me. And then, "I wish there was something that could improve my eyesight." And then, "When are we going to go shopping for that new computer?"

"Well, let's make sure you can see the screen first," I say, which sounds cruel, but she has complained to me tonight that she wasn't able to see any of the words on her screen, though I think this has less to do with her eyesight than the glasses she's wearing. Unnaturally thick and foggy. My mother looks foggy, too, almost drunk, disheveled in her dirty sweater, though she doesn't drink. It's probably the medicine she's been taking for her many conditions. My mother owns at least half a dozen glasses, and I know I should have sorted through them all by now (we tried once), but so many things have gone wrong in the last five months since my mother moved to Bellingham that sorting through her glasses is a side issue. I get up from the couch in the cramped living room of her apartment, step over the coffee table—careful not to tip over the cup of peppermint tea I'm drinking out of a beer stein, careful not to bump into my mother—and cross to the bedroom crammed with wardrobe boxes and too much furniture, though much less than what she's used to. On her dresser there are parts of various eyeglasses: maimed glasses, the corpses of eyeglasses, a dark orphaned lens here, a frame there, an empty case, and one case with a pair that's whole. This is the one I grab and take out to my mother, who is waiting patiently, always patient these days, or perhaps so unnerved and exhausted that it passes for patience. She takes the case from me and takes off the old glasses, places them beside her beer mug of licorice tea, and puts on the new pair.

She rubs an eye, says, "This seems to be helping. Maybe these are my reading glasses." I should know, of course. I should have had them color-coded by now, but I haven't yet.

She bends down to the photo from the newsletter on the coffee table and says, "Yes, that's William Carlos Williams."

A little earlier she told me about the photo. "It's in one of those boxes," she told me. "I saw it the other day. I thought I'd told you about it before," but she hadn't, this photo of her with William Carlos Williams, Theodore Roethke, and other famous writers. So I spent fifteen minutes rifling through her boxes of bills and old papers mixed up on the kitchen counter (a Cascade Gas Company bill, final payment requested for service at the apartment she moved into in December, when we still thought she could live on her own; a letter from the superintendent of public schools of New York City, dated 1959, addressed to my grandmother, a teacher at the time, telling her how many sick days she was allowed), looking for the photo, until she explained that it was actually part of a newsletter from the artists' colony Yaddo, in Saratoga Springs, New York. Armed with that crucial bit of information, I found it.

The photo is captioned "Class picture, 1950."

"Can you pick me out?" she says.

From left, top: William Osborne, Theodore Roethke, Robel Paris, Harvey Shapiro, Elaine Gottlieb, Beryl Levy, Cid Corman, Simmons Persons, Gladys Farnel, Hans Sahl, Clifford Wright, Richard Eberhart. From left, bottom: Ben Weber, Nicholas Callas, Jessamyn West, Eugenie Gershoy, William Carlos Williams, Flossie Williams, Mitsu Yashima, Charles Schucker, Elizabeth Ames, John Dillon Husband.

Not many of these people are smiling. Eugenie Gershoy, seated next to Jessamyn West, has a little smirk, and Mitsu Yashima, seated next to Flossie Williams, smiles broadly, and also Cid Corman in the back row, whom I met in 1975 when I was a high school exchange student in Japan. My mother visited me in Osaka and we traveled by train to Kyoto, to Cid Corman's ice cream parlor, where I ate a hamburger, had an ice cream cone, and listened to a poetry reading while my mother and Cid reminisced.

"Don't I look prim?" my mother says, and she does. Or maybe it's something else. Scared? Intimidated? Shocked? My mother was thirty-four then—this was a year or so before she met my father. My sister, Nola, was three, and my mother was an up-and-coming young writer, one novel published in 1947. John Crowe Ransom liked her work, publishing several of her stories in the *Kenyon Review*. I wasn't born until 1958.

She stands up straight, hands behind her back, a scarf tied loosely around her neck, draping down over a breast, a flower pinned to the scarf. Theodore Roethke stands, huge, imposing, dour. In an accompanying article Harvey Shapiro tells of how publicly Roethke liked to display his wounds, how he told Shapiro of his hurt that John Crowe Ransom had rejected "My Papa's Waltz," though Roethke was famous by then and the poem had been widely anthologized. What remained, still, was Roethke's pain, perhaps the pain of rejection meshed with the pain of the poem's subject matter—abuse at the hands of his drunken father. Shapiro also tells of Roethke's claim that he'd bummed his way to Yaddo after escaping in drag from a mental institution on the west coast earlier that summer. "He liked to romanticize his mental illness," Shapiro writes. Perhaps, but something honest still comes across in that picture, the despair clear for anyone to view head-on.

In the front row, William Carlos Williams sits cross-legged, dignified.

"He dreamed of my legs," my mother tells me.

"William Carlos Williams dreamed of your legs?" I ask.

"At breakfast one day he said he'd had a dream about my legs. 'That girl has nice legs,' he said."

We have to keep going back over histories, our own and the histories of others, constantly revising. There's no single truth . . . except that, perhaps. History is not always recorded and not always written by the victor. History is not always written. We carry our secret histories behind our words, in another room, in the eyeglass case on the dresser in the bedroom. Maybe someone comes along and finds the right pair. Maybe we have too many, unsorted.

My mother's former landlord, Loyce, wants to know the history of the "L." I was gone for the past week in Hawaii, and that's the only reason I haven't called before now. Loyce has left messages on my answering machine twice, ostensibly to see about getting back my mother's deposit to us—minus a charge for mowing, the ad for renting the apartment again, a reasonable charge for her time, and of course, for painting over the "L." She'd also like the keys back from us. But the "L" is the real reason she's called. My mother wrote an "L" on the wall of the apartment in indelible magic marker before she left. "I'm dying to know the story," Loyce says. "I know there's a good story behind it."

Loyce appreciates a good story, and this is one of the things I appreciate about Loyce, that and her compassion. She moved to Bellingham several years ago to take care of her ailing mother, and now lives in her mother's old house on top of a hill with a view of the bay and the San Juan Islands. So she understands our situation. She knows that my mother can't live alone anymore, that all of us were taken by surprise by her condition when she moved here five months ago. Until then, my mother had been living on her own in South Bend, Indiana, where she taught writing until ten years ago. She'd been living on her own since I moved out at the age of sixteen to go to boarding school, and had been taking care of herself since 1966 when my father died. But in the last several months things have fallen apart. Our first inkling was the mover, a man in his sixties who worked with his son. He took me aside on the first day and told me that in his thirty years of moving he'd never seen an apartment as messy as my mother's.

When he and his son went to my mom's apartment in South Bend, they almost turned around.

"You don't have to do this if you don't want," the mover told his son.

No, the first inkling was my brother's call from L.A., where my mother was visiting a few days prior to her big move. The van had loaded in South Bend and she'd flown off to L.A. to visit him and his family. The night before her flight from L.A. to Seattle he called me near midnight and said, "Mom's hallucinating."

I asked him what he meant, what she was seeing, and he told me that she was seeing all these people who didn't exist and making strange remarks. "When I picked her up at the airport, she said there was a group of Asians having a baby. She said they were a troupe of actors and they were doing a skit."

Still, the next day, he put her on the plane to me, and I picked her up and brought her to her new home. Since then, we have gone to three different doctors and my mother has had brain scans and blood tests and sonograms of her carotid arteries and been placed on a small dose of an anti-psychotic drug. One doctor says her cerebral cortex has shrunk and she's had a series of tiny strokes to individual arteries in her brain.

At three A.M. one morning, the police call me up and tell me that my mother thinks someone is trying to break into her apartment.

"Is there anyone living with her?" the policeman asks.

"No."

"She says a handicapped woman lives with her. You might want to see a doctor about this."

I take her to doctors and try to convince my mother that she needs to live where she can be safe, but she refuses to even consider it. "I should have stayed in New York," she tells me. "I never should have left." And then, "I should never have come here. Why can't you be on my side?" And then, "I'll move down to L.A. Your brother is much nicer than you are."

I spend a few nights at her apartment, and she tells me about the Middle Eastern couple who have taken over her bedroom and the children who are there, and the landlord comes over and puts a lock on the door from the kitchen to the garage, though we know no one was trying to break in. And homeless people are living on her back porch. And she keeps startling people in the garage who are removing her belongings.

But finally.

After my cousin David flies up from L.A. After visiting a dozen managed-care facilities, after my brother says he thinks it's the medicine that's doing this and I talk to the doctors and the doctors talk to each other and they talk to my mother and she says, "The doctor says I'm fine," and I say, "No, he doesn't," and she hangs up, turns off her hearing aid.

And coincidentally, a friend of my mother's in South Bend wins second place in a poetry competition run by the literary journal I edit. The poems were all anonymous, and I had nothing to do with the judging, but my mother's friend has won second prize for a poem about her delusional mother, called "My Mother and Dan Rather." I call her up to tell her the good news of her award, but she assumes, of course, I'm calling to talk about my mother. So that's what we do for half an hour. She tells me she's distanced herself over the last year from my mother because she seemed too much like her own mother, and she tells me that several of my mother's friends wondered if they should call me and let me know what was going on.

I almost forget to tell her about her prize.

No, the first inkling was two years ago. My wife, Beverly, wondered aloud about my mother's memory, her hold on reality. I told Beverly my mother had always been kind of scattered, messy, unfocused.

And finally. After I come into her apartment one day and feel the heat. I go to the stove and turn off the glowing burners. My mother has a blister on her hand the size of a walnut. Beverly tells me that it's insane for my mother to live alone, that somehow we have to force her to move. "What if she sets the apartment on fire? She might not only kill herself, but the people next door."

"I know," I tell her. "I'm trying." But I also know that short of a court order, short of being declared her legal guardian, I can't force her.

And finally. I convince my mother to come with me to the Leopold, a historic hotel in downtown Bellingham that has been converted into apartments for seniors, one wing assisted living, the other independent. We have lunch there one day. My mother likes the food.

And finally, she agrees to spend a couple of weeks there in a guest room.

Famous people stayed at the Leopold, I tell my mother. Rutherford B. Hayes. Jenny Lind, the Swedish Nightingale. This doesn't impress her, of course. She has known more famous people than can fit on a plaque. But she has a nice view of the bay, somewhat blocked by the Georgia Pacific Paper Mill. And she likes the food but the apartment is only two cramped rooms, and across the street at the Greek restaurant, people party until two each night and climb trees and conduct military rituals. And the Iraqi army rolled through the streets one night. And a truck dumped two bodies, a man and a woman dressed in formal evening attire.

"They sometimes flood the parking lot," she tells me, "and use it as a waterway."

Or, "Look at that," pointing, reaching for nothing.

She keeps returning to the apartment, driven by the woman I've hired to clean it. My mother wants to drive again, and I tell her no, she can't possibly, and I read articles and watch programs that tell me not to reverse roles, not to become the parent, and I wonder how that's possible to avoid. One day, I walk into her apartment and find signs she's posted all around on the bed, in the guest room, on the kitchen counter. "Keep off." "Stay out." "Go Away." I ask her about these signs and she tells me they're just a joke. She's become wary of me. I tell her she's safe, ask her why she feels so threatened. She tells me, "I've never felt safe in my life."

During this period, my mother writes her "L" on the wall of the kitchen.

And the weeks at the Leopold have turned to months, and now most of her belongings are stuffed into a heated mini-storage unit. More of her belongings are stuffed into the basement of the Leopold.

Finally.

I almost don't want to tell Loyce the story of the "L" when she calls. I'd like to keep her in suspense, because sometimes that's stronger than the truth. She probably thinks it's about her, that the "L" stands for Loyce, but it doesn't. It stands for Leopold. One day my mother was at the apartment, after we finally convinced her she had to move, and I gave her a magic marker and asked her to mark the boxes she'd like taken to the Leopold. Apparently, she thought she was marking a box, but she was really marking the wall. This is what she really wanted. That was not lost on me. She loved that apartment. She wanted her independence, but this was just too much for me to move.

Loyce and I say goodbye after I assure her I'll return the keys and she assures me she'll return most of the deposit. It's already eight-thirty and I told my mother I'd be over around eight, but I had to read to my kids first. I haven't seen them in a week. I've just returned from Hawaii.

In Hawaii, where I've been researching a new book, I probably had more fun than I should have. Not the kind of fun with life-bending consequences, but fun nonetheless, hanging out with a former student, eating out every night, smoking cigars, drinking. For ten dollars a day more, I was told at the airport, I could rent a convertible—a Ford Mustang, or a Caddie, and I'm not ready for that, so I take the Mustang. Stupid. The wife of the friend I'm staying with laughed when she saw it in her driveway. "Oh," she tells me. "I thought maybe Robbie was having a mid-life crisis." No, it's me probably, even though I hate to admit it. I refuse to believe such a thing could happen to me at this preordained age, a month from forty, that I could be saddled with such a cliché crisis, such mediocre regrets.

Olivia wants to read to me tonight, all seven stories from an Arnold Lobel book. "They're short," she assures me. We compromise on three, her three favorites. One of these she read last week to her class while I was in Hawaii. Beverly, who sometimes works in Olivia's class as a volunteer, has already told me that the class was enthralled by Olivia. "She acted so confident. She took her time and showed them the pictures."

The one she read to her class, "The Journey," is about a mouse who wants to visit his mother, and in a sequence of transactions, acquires a car, roller skates, boots, sneakers, and finally a new set of feet. When he reaches his mother she hugs him, kisses him, and says, "Hello, my son, you are looking fine—and what nice new feet you have!" Olivia's whole class broke out in hysterical laughter, she assured me.

I've brought my mother a box of chocolate-covered macadamia nuts. She looks at it, bewildered. "Oh, I thought it was a book," she says.

I make tea for us, but she only has a few tea mugs and they're dirty, so we have to use beer steins. "I've ended up with such an odd assortment of things," she tells me, and she blames this on the movers.

A week before my trip to Hawaii, I visited her and she showed me a notebook in which she'd kept a journal during the mid-seventies. My mother has kept journals from the time she was sixteen, a series of secret histories written in any notebook she could find. But now, she cannot read these histories, and she asks me to read this one to her.

"I might use it in a story," she tells me. "It's about Moe and Helen." Moe is Moe Howard, of the Three Stooges. He was a cousin of ours by marriage, and whenever she visited California, she'd stop by to see them. Moe, who had such a violent on-screen persona: Think of him saying, "Wise guy, eh?" Poking the eyes of Larry, Curly, Shemp, or one of the later pseudo-Stooges, Curly Joe and Joe Besser. I met him once, a frail old man with white hair, too quiet to seem like Moe. Off-screen, he was a gentle family man, kind and grateful to his fans, never refusing to sign an autograph. What my mother wants me to read to her is an account of the last time she saw Moe and his wife Helen, when they were both dying.

> Seeing Moe and Helen was touching—a beautiful hill of purple flowers outside that Moe said was all theirs—a beautifully furnished, expensively comfortable house through which they glide, ghost-like. They don't kiss me because of the possibility of germs. Helen is in a loose purple nylon dressing gown. She has been recuperating from a breast operation and says in a slightly quaking voice that she will be going to the doctor soon and will probably have cobalt. . . .
>
> Moe is red-faced and very thin. His thinness, wispiness, makes him look elfin—because he used to be heavier, he seemed bigger. His hair is white. He smiles proudly, talking about his appearances at colleges and his memoirs which comprise many books. Talk about the film I am supposed to have made with him. He reminds me that I acted in it (at the age of about 19) 8mm, I think, with his children. But it is packed somewhere with thousands of feet of other film.

As I'm reading this to my mother I feel odd, wondering if she notices the similarities between this passage and her own present life—the things packed away, the memories, the frailty—but I say nothing about this, though it moves me. Instead, I ask her about this film she was in, and she tells me it was an impromptu home movie in which Moe was cast as the villain, of course, and she was the protector of his children. She has never seen it, but it exists somewhere. Moe's daughter, Joan, once showed me the huge roll of home movies in her attic. Towards the end of his life, Moe took every home movie he made and spliced them all together onto one monstrous cumbersome roll that no one could ever possibly watch in its entirety. Somewhere on this roll exists a movie with my mother, age nineteen, circa 1935.

Silently, I flip through other pages in my mother's journal, as she sits near me, lost in her memories, needing no journal really.

I am not in fantasyland. I am painfully living out my loneliness and nostalgia. I dream of my son every night and wish he were here. Those who have died are intolerably absent and I feel that all the love I need and want will not come because I had my chance and lost it, and what man will be responsible for or will react to my aging, my passion, my intolerable loneliness . . . ?

I am with her now, but not. We see each other through veils. We have battled for this moment, and neither sees the other as we would like.

William Carlos Williams dreamed of my mother's legs, as did other men that summer of 1950 at Yaddo.

As we bend over the class photo, circa 1950, she tells me the official history of that summer, how special it was for her, how it was so exciting to be around such vital intellects, such talented writers. "It was really something, going down to breakfast and having conversations with all these people. The talent was never quite the same after that."

I tell her I'd love to have a copy of this picture. "You could write to Yaddo," she says. "They use it for publicity." She tells me I could write to one of the writers pictured with her. "It's the least he could do," she says, with what seems like bitterness, and I let this remark wash over me because I think I know what's behind it.

Once, a number of years ago, Beverly and my mother and I were on a drive, and I was telling her about a friend of mine who'd done his dissertation on the poetry of one of the poets pictured in the photo. From the back seat my mother blurted, "You know, he raped me."

Beverly and I looked at one another. We didn't say anything. We didn't know what to say. The remark was so sudden, so unexpected, we hardly knew how to react. We were silent, all three of us. Neither Beverly nor I mentioned this to each other later.

My mother starts talking about him now, though I haven't asked. She says, "One time, he invited me to a private party, and innocent that I was, I went there." In memory, she's lucid. Only the present is slippery, tricky, untrustworthy.

"There were all these men there. They were all leches. Ted Roethke kept lunging for me, just making grabs. He really had problems," and she laughs. She mentions the name of the poet who was her friend, whom she trusted. He was younger than her, than all these other famous men. "I thought he'd protect me." She laughs again. This time, there's no mistaking the bitterness.

I think about asking her. What term to use? "He assaulted you?"

"Yes," she says.

"Did it happen at Yaddo?" I ask.

She nods.

"Did you ever confront him?"

"No," she says. "I don't want to talk about it."

But then she says, "There wasn't much I could do. In those days, there wasn't much to do. I just pretended it didn't happen. For a little while, he became my boyfriend."

I don't know what to say. I probably shouldn't say anything. I sigh. "He should have been locked up. How could he be your boyfriend after that?"

"He was drunk when it happened," and I want to say that's no excuse, but I keep my mouth shut and let her talk. "I left the party early and he followed me back to my room. I tried to lock the door, but the lock was broken.

"I turned things around. I had to. I was confused. In my mind, he became my protector from the other men there."

I study the picture again. My mother's expression and the expressions of the men. I wonder when this photo was taken, before or after the assault my mother describes. The photo has taken on the quality of a group mug shot to me. I think they look like jerks, most of them—except for Cid Corman, who my mother says is a wonderful person, and maybe some others, too, maybe William Carlos Williams, who dreamed of my mother's legs and "had an eye for the ladies" as my mother says. Maybe even dour Theodore Roethke, though he lunged at her as though she was something being wheeled by on a dessert tray.

"They weren't famous for their personalities," she tells me.

I think about these people in the photo; how unfair it seems to me that someone can go on to have a career, hide behind his smirk, have dissertations written about him, how the actions of some people seem to have no visible consequences. I think of my mother's secret histories, her journals, her blurted comments, her assertion that she has never felt safe.

I flip the newsletter over to the section titled "Recent Works Produced by Yaddo Fellows," and see that the latest works reported are from 1987. For an absurd moment, I believe that none of the Fellows at Yaddo have been productive for over ten years, and this makes me happy, but then I realize the newsletter itself is ten years old.

My mother has taken to carrying a picture of me—Ideal Robin, I call it—skinny, sitting languorously, smiling beside a life-size cardboard cutout of Rudolph Valentino. The son she longed for in her journal perhaps hardly exists anymore—I was away at boarding school that year, my choice, not hers, and I never returned.

I have come to visit her now. I've knocked lightly. I've used my key. She can barely see me when I walk into her apartment. I've told her I've returned from Hawaii, that she can expect me around eight, but I'm late and as I push open the door she's looking at me almost suspiciously, because really her eyesight is that bad, and until I speak she has no idea who's entering. The Iraqi army? A stranger who wants her belongings? A poet she thinks is her "protector" but means her harm? I half expect to see signs, "Keep Off," "Stay Out," "Go Away." I have brought a box of chocolate-covered macadamia nuts. I am wearing new feet, but she doesn't notice. Tomorrow she will have surgery on her eyes that will not improve anything, but keep things from getting worse. How much worse could things get for this woman who loves words, but can neither see nor write them anymore? Does her history go on inside her, on some gigantic roll of spliced-together home movies? Tell me the story of the "L." Tell me the story of the wall of your apartment. Tell me the story of those talented writers who publicly display their wounds and the writers who secretly wound others. Tell me which is worse. She kisses me lightly and I give her her gift. And she says, once, only once, though I keep hearing it, the disappointment, and strangely, even fear, "Oh, I thought it was a book."

Interview with Robin Hemley

1. The use of lenses and seeing the truth is a good technique, especially when coupled with the number of revisions to how your mother's demise began. Assuming you have more hindsight after writing this essay, is there anything you see now that you didn't see then?

Generally, I think it's best to have some distance when writing about something difficult and/or traumatic—that's something I often tell my students. But this piece was written in the moment, as I was experiencing my mother's descent into dementia. I was quite close to my mother and so this was a difficult piece to write, and to this day, sixteen years after it was first written, the piece still feels rather raw to me. I can't really say that I see anything differently now, or that I would have added anything or left anything out. This was one of those organic pieces that seemed in retrospect to write itself.

2. It is implied that you believe your mother was assaulted, as she is able to think clearly in memory, just not in the present. Did you ever doubt your mom's story?

I probably did doubt my mother's story at one time or another. She was essentially a private person, but on occasion she'd blurt out something dramatic at times that didn't always seem appropriate. My adolescent sense of embarrassment lingered well into my twenties and thirties—unfairly to my mother, I'm sure. While essentially she was quite an honest person, she was prone to self-dramatizing, but I'm quite certain of her story, nonetheless. I have no proof that the man she said assaulted her—whom I didn't actually name in the essay—did indeed assault her. The story had the ring of truth when she told it to me and certainly fit the attitudes of the egoistic male writers of the era. My mother was something of a pioneer in that the literary world was definitely an old boy's club in the 1950s, when the assault took place, and the sense of entitlement that these guys had was unbelievable by today's standards. The poet Cid Corman, whom she met at Yaddo during that visit, was an exception—he was the ONLY guy there who wasn't hitting on her. Sexual assaults aren't a thing of the past, by any means, far from it, but attitudes and laws are different now, and at least it's somewhat less likely that such a scenario would play out now as it did in my mother's day at Yaddo.

3. The structure of the piece is circular. How does this structure help tell the secret and assist you in coming to terms with your grief?

Grief is a recursive thing—just as my mother replayed her life and disappointments on an endless tape loop in her mind, so, too, I saw the form as imitative of this state. And I certainly felt caught in something of an endless cycle of my own grief at the loss of the mother I had once known.

4. What advice do you have for beginning writers who are trying to find the "right glasses" through which to see their families, their past, and their stories?

I think it's important not to be your own worst censor. Too often when people write about their families, they worry too much about how they will be attacked or criticized or shunned by their family members. My feeling is that it's important to get the story down as you see it—if it's a family story, my feeling is that you have part ownership of it in that these family stories help shape who you are. I've written a lot about my family—and that surprises me in hindsight, because I never would have thought that I would write so much about them—my birth family and my own children—when I was a young writer. For better or worse, this is what I've done. For the most part, despite my fears in the past about family reactions, my family has seen my writing as a kind of family chronicle—and you have to be honest about these things. The big myth about any family is that any family is perfect. But there's no perfect family, just as there's no perfect person, and writers should not be in the business of perpetuating lies and self-perpetuating myths. The family almost always has a vested interest in creating an overarching narrative of itself, but most of these narratives are actually counterproductive and simply lock in familial delusions and destructive behaviors. I think that most of my family understands this. My two eldest daughters both gave one of my memoirs to their boyfriends so that they would better understand us—that's really gratifying to me. So I think it's always important to write honestly about your family, but that means that you have to write honestly about yourself. This doesn't mean that one's writing needs always to be confessional or revealing of skeletons in the closet. There are many other smaller ways in which to be untruthful about oneself and one's family, and these small elisions are as important as the big ones.

Leaving Duck Creek

Mary Clearman Blew

By the time my little sister and I enrolled in the Duck Creek School in 1949, a lot in ranch country had changed. For one thing, the terrible drought years of the 1920s and the depression of the 1930s had ended the hopes of thousands of young homesteaders, who lost their farms and ranches to debt and foreclosure. Montana lost a third of its population during those years, and over half of its rural schools. Then came World War II and another population shift, giving rural teachers like my favorite aunt the chance to move over to Washington State and earn twice the salary without having to shovel coal and carry water. Rural school boards searched high and low, but if they couldn't find a teacher, the school had to close.

Not that I understood anything about history or economics, but I did overhear some of the anxious conversation—Have you found a teacher yet? No, have you?

But the day came when my little sister and I, decked out in new dresses hand sewn by my mother and equipped with a new lunch box to share and new tablets and pencils and crayons, were driven up the precarious dirt road from the ranch and over several miles of graveled road to the Duck Creek School.

September in Montana can be dry and mild, and I remember our introduction to Duck Creek as very pleasant. The school was fresh from its fall cleaning, and the American flag floated from its pole, and the windows had been opened to the familiar odors of ripening wheat and creek water. So many novelties to experience: a hallway with hooks for our coats and a Redwing cooler that held drinking water, the long schoolroom with rows of desks in graduated sizes, the portraits of George Washington and Abraham Lincoln on the wall above the teacher's desk, and most enticing of all, a three-shelf bookcase that was the school's library.

Including my sister and me, nine pupils were enrolled in the Duck Creek School that fall: the three Anderson girls, who rode horseback down from their father's remote ranch in the foothills and stabled their horses in the ramshackle barn during the school day; Buzzie Huffine, a large and good-natured seventh-grader; Louise Snapp and her brother Billy, who were attending the Duck Creek School because their parents hadn't been able to find a teacher for their school; and Dixie Grover, who would be a first-grader with my sister.

There were other pleasures. Games at recess that involved kicking cans or choosing up sides and running back and forth with sticks from the woodpile. Taking turns carrying the water bucket across the gravel road in front of the school, over the stile, and down the trail to the spring in the cow pasture to fetch back water to pour into the Redwing cooler. I knew that my favorite aunt had taught at the Duck Creek School in the dim past—she'd actually taught the oldest Anderson girl as a first-grader—but I didn't know she had noted in her diary the day she had followed that same trail through the cow pasture to clean that same spring. I hadn't grasped the unspoken family assumption that I would follow in her and my mother's footsteps and teach in my own country school someday. But I was changing. The days when I thought of myself in third person were long past; wary of ridicule from listening adults, I no longer told myself out loud what I was thinking. I was on the cusp of a new awareness, seeing the world through my own eyes and no one else's, and my eyes were on that case of unread books. I wouldn't stop until I had finished every single book, and then I would start reading them all over again.

Those days at Duck Creek sometimes seem as close and immediate and clear as the glass of those tall schoolhouse windows that looked across the trampled grass of the schoolyard to the graveled road angling north toward the Judith Mountains and eventually fading out of sight. The schoolroom itself was like a capsule in which routines were repeated day after day and nothing exciting happened, except the day the stubble field on the other side of the schoolyard caught fire and one of the Anderson girls jumped on her horse and tore off to get help from a neighbor while the teacher and Buzzie Huffine beat back the flames with shovels and sacks.

In the capsule of the schoolroom, with its pinewood floors and interlocking desks with lids that lifted over the clutter of our workbooks, as we scratched away with the steel pens that were passed out at penmanship time, and breathed the fumes of real ink, we lived in the present, with little suspicion of a future and no sense of the past as anything but remote. We didn't know that we were the last generation of children to dip our steel pens into our little bottles of reeking ink and practice slants and ovals on lined paper, according to the Palmer method, with admonitions from the teacher not to draw our ovals with our fingers (lest writer's cramp set in) but to keep our hands and wrists motionless and move our pens by rotating our forearms on our desks. As we obediently dipped our pens and rotated our forearms, we were anachronisms ranging in age from five to seventeen, but we didn't know it.

Our teacher that first year was a short-tempered redhead who drove out from Lewistown on Monday mornings, spent the week in the teacherage behind the schoolroom, and drove back to Lewistown on Friday afternoons to spend the weekend with her husband. Neighborhood gossip had it that she was teaching to keep ahead of his gambling debts. I can't remember any of the lessons she taught, although I do remember her scolding me for reading too fast, or not reading closely—"I was watching your eyes! They weren't moving back and forth across the lines! Read it again!"

She was right about the way my eyes moved on the page. I had taught myself to read in a kind of sweep, in the literary equivalent of bolting my food. I had been tested that summer by the county superintendent of schools so she could decide which grade I should be placed in, although discovering that I was reading at a twelfth-grade level and doing arithmetic at a third-grade level couldn't have been much help to her. It didn't matter to me when I was placed in fourth grade with two of the Anderson girls and Billy Snapp. They couldn't keep up with me. I finished what I was assigned and then I reread one of the seventy or so books that made up the school library, or I sat and drew pictures, or I entertained myself with my elaborately imagined stories that spun through my head like an alternative life I was living. The redheaded teacher was the least of my worries.

I now suspect that I was the least of hers. If I wasn't going to pay attention to what she was trying to teach me, she may have decided I wasn't worth the bother. She hadn't wanted my little sister and me in her school in the first place. Like Louise and Billy Snapp, we belonged in another district, except that in our case our assigned school was situated on the other side of the Judith River, with no bridge for miles. But there we were in the Duck Creek School, and there was the redheaded teacher, and when my five-year-old sister threw up because the teacher yelled at her for forgetting the words on the page, she gave up on my sister, too. It wasn't until my sister started in a Lewistown school in the middle of fourth grade that anyone realized she had never learned to read at all.

Thanks to my valiant rancher grandmother, who drilled and drilled me, I learned the multiplication tables and I learned to spell. My rancher grandmother also cared deeply about the doings of people like Coronado and Cortez and de Soto and de León, and she tried to interest me in the string of firsts they seemed to have run up, like discovering the Mississippi River and the Fountain of Youth, but in that project she was never successful.

My sister and I attended the Duck Creek School for three and a half years. A well-meaning little woman with two sons of her own had followed the redheaded woman as our teacher, but it was during that final half year that we learned just how strange school could be.

It had looked as though we wouldn't find a teacher for that final year at all. Then—hallelujah!—at the last possible minute, a neighboring ranch wife said she'd take the school. She'd been very ill—she wasn't sure she could do it—but yes, she thought she could. Everyone was very pleased; she was said to have been an excellent teacher before her illness.

Years later I wrote a short story about those few months with the teacher I called Mrs. Skaarda, and when the story was published in the *Georgia Review*, my sister and brother-in-law read it.

"She had to have made it up. These things couldn't have happened," said my brother-in-law.

"Oh yes they did," said my sister. "Oh yes they did."

Mrs. Skaarda, as I'll continue to call her, was a bird-boned little woman with an anxious face, and eyes that searched our faces for reassurance as she told us how glad she was to be well again, and how much she looked forward to be spending the year with us. We were a depleted little group; the oldest Anderson girl had turned eighteen and given up on schooling, and Buzzie and his mother had moved to town after his father died, and the Snapps, miraculously, had found a teacher for their school, so Billy and Louise were gone. Besides my sister and me, that left only the other two Andersons and two new first-graders, a little girl I'll now call Jill, who seemed to have a bladder infection, and a little boy whom I called Forby in my short story.

All of us except Jill and Forby were surprised when Mrs. Skaarda didn't assign us schoolwork, but instead began a rambling monologue from which, she said, she hoped we learned more than we would from lessons. What she wanted us to know was that she had enemies. There had been professors when she was in college, the director of a theater group she had belonged to, a man who had taught her niece so badly in a city school, her sister-in-law . . .

It turned out that her father-in-law had been dying of cancer. Mrs. Skaarda's voice shook as she told us how cancer had its own terrible smell, so putrid and horrible that only she, of the whole family, could bear to sit in the same room with him. Others in the family, she said, didn't really *care* that he was dying.

At this point Jill flung herself out of her seat and tore through the schoolroom, banging doors behind her, on her way to the outhouse.

Mrs. Skaarda went on talking about her father-in-law. Her voice trembled. "I sat up with him all night. I held his hand. No one else would stay with him. He died about three o'clock in the morning. Did you know that dead bodies fart?"

We sat in rapt silence, all but Forby, who was coloring with his black crayon.

As the fall grew chillier and the oil stove had to be lit, Mrs. Skaarda grew fearful. After a few days of ordinary lessons, her eyes searched the classroom and came to rest on the stove.

"If it exploded, it would kill us all." Her voice broke the silence, and we all looked up, blinking in the sunlight that strained through the frosted windows. All but Forby, that is, who kept coloring with his black crayon. "My desk is on the far side of the room, and they might be able to identify my body. But most of you would be mutilated beyond recognition."

"If it exploded, I'd jump up and run," said one of the Anderson girls.

"You wouldn't have time to run," said Mrs. Skaarda.

For the rest of the week we watched the oil heater and breathed as tentatively as we could. Mrs. Skaarda, however, had begun to worry about Jill, who continued to punctuate her runs to the outhouse with slammed doors.

"She's been wetting her panties," said Mrs. Skaarda. "I can smell her."

Slam! went another door behind one of Jill's desperate dashes.

"Bang! Bang!" Mrs. Skaarda shouted at the slammed door. "There go the British!"

We never knew what became of Jill. She simply stopped attending school. It is possible that Mrs. Skaarda complained to her parents, or more likely to the neighbors who had hired her parents for fall work. Or maybe Jill told her parents what was happening. Or maybe not; maybe her family just moved away. When I look back over those years, I'm struck by how little any of us told our parents about what was happening at school. We chattered at home about who said what smart thing on the playground and what smart thing got said back, but we didn't tell that my sister threw up when the redheaded teacher yelled at her, or that the redheaded teacher once sneaked up behind me and pummeled me with her fists for no reason I ever knew, and we didn't tell about Mrs. Skaarda until long after the fact.

Did our complicit silence grow out of our sense of the schoolroom as a capsule in which we were suspended from the day-to-day of the rest of the world? As I reread my short story, I am struck by what I kept of the facts and what I changed: my own role in the Forby episode, for example.

Because, after Jill vanished, Mrs. Skaarda turned her attention on Forby. "There's something the matter with him," she whispered to the rest of us. "Why does he always color with his black crayon?"

Forby kept coloring, and Mrs. Skaarda's worries grew. "If he were ever to lose control, it would take more than any one of us to subdue him," she confided in her troubled whisper. "The insane have strength beyond all normal measures. That's what I'm afraid of. That he'll snap and overpower us all."

By this time every pair of eyes in school was glued on Forby. Could we possibly have believed the child was insane? I only know that Forby gradually looked up from his crayons to find a wall of suspicion around him. At recess he was no longer chosen on anyone's side in games. He took to hovering at a distance of a few yards, pawing with his overshoes at the sod.

"Get away!" somebody might bellow across a few yards of prairie grass at uncomprehending Forby in his thick coat and cap. "Keep away from us!"

"Go away!"

From the first, Forby made no defense, withdrawing more deeply into himself when we darted at him, threatening. How long did our bullying go on? Could it have been for days? And what part did I play, what am I masking from myself by my use of the collective "we," my sheltering in our tiny group? I do remember that the day Forby finally broke and ran, I ran after him with everybody else, and just as we saw we were going to corner him by the barbed wire fence that separated the schoolyard from the neighboring grain field, Forby flung himself on that fence and set the wires vibrating for yards.

At that precise moment, Forby's mother showed up. She broke into a run with her coat flapping about her legs, plucked Forby off the barbed wire, and carried him back toward the school.

Here my memory darkens. I cannot see Forby lolling on her shoulder as she opens the door of the school; I cannot see her carrying him to her car. Her arrival seemed to me at the time as just one more unlikely event. Was it in fact a complete non sequitur, or had she gotten wind of the bullying and come to look into it? I do know that I was eleven and the Anderson girls probably twelve and fourteen, old enough to know we shouldn't have been picking on a six-year-old.

In my short story, my point-of-view character is a revision of myself as Forby's prime persecutor, whose motive is to win Mrs. Skaarda's approval. I can gloss my revision as a way of telling the story of a scapegoat, or I can ponder the story I was avoiding, because at the time, the last thing on my mind was Mrs. Skaarda's approval. In retrospect, I realize that growing between us was the perverse flower of antagonism that I would feel toward various teachers and professors even through graduate school. Mrs. Skaarda and I argued about the interpretations of stories in school readers. We argued about the correct position of one's fingers on piano keys (I was taking piano lessons from the redoubtable Miss Pennock in Lewistown, who insisted on a certain finger curvature and wrist position that Mrs. Skaarda considered unnecessary and ungraceful). We argued about the significance of ancient Mayan human sacrifice (a detail I retained in my short story was that she lent me a book on the topic that gave me nightmares). Mouthy and obnoxious, that was me—or, at least, how Mrs. Skaarda probably saw me.

Our days at Duck Creek were coming to an end. The first winter blizzard hit just as my parents began to move from the ranch on the river to the ranch they had bought in the foothills of the Snowy Mountains, close enough to Lewistown that my sister and I, and the new little sister, ten years younger than I, could attend town schools and eventually go to high school without having to board away from home. What with the perils of bad roads and blowing snow and the uncertainties of starting over, my father and mother would have had more on their minds than Mrs. Skaarda and the shadows only she perceived.

But I missed a day or two of school, toward the end of that last term, and my little sister uncharacteristically came home with a story about Mrs. Skaarda, who had gathered her dwindling little flock about her and told them that Mary hated her.

"But you"—she smiled through her tears, hugging my sister—"you're so sweet. You'd do anything for me."

The Duck Creek School couldn't have stayed open for more than another year or two, if that. For a long time it sat empty by the side of the road, its long row of windows filmed with dust, until somebody hauled it off to use as a granary. Mrs. Skaarda got a job teaching in an elementary school in a small town and won a Teacher of the Year award. The youngest Anderson girl gave high school a try and dropped out after a few months. Forby grew up to farm his father's land. Jill might as well have dropped off the face of the earth, as far as any of us ever knew.

A fourth-grade teacher in Lewistown spotted my sister's illiteracy and taught her to read. I started high school with a curious assortment of knowledge and skills—the multiplication tables; an unwilling suspicion that de Soto, de León, Cortez, and Coronado really mattered; and the ability to read faster than anyone my teachers had ever encountered—and found in those teachers a whole new set of assumptions about what a girl ought to learn, and how she ought to learn it.

Several years ago my sister and I detoured off the highway, now a paved road, and visited the granary that once had been the Duck Creek School. It tilted off its foundation with its desks still bolted to its hardwood floor and a clutter of forgotten primers and workbooks discarded in the chaff. My sister picked up one of the readers as a keepsake, then changed her mind, laid it back down on the floor, and took a few pictures instead. It seemed the right thing to do. Those pictures show us in our bright summer clothing, a couple of aliens in a dusty time capsule. And yet that time capsule, lopsided and askew, once had been solid and real and eternal. Mrs. Skaarda was right: we had learned a great deal at Duck Creek that had nothing to do with lessons.

Interview with Mary Clearman Blew

1. In the first half of the essay, you mention the decision to keep secret (or at least keep to yourself) the "stories that spun through my head like an

alternative life I was living." As an adult, do you still have that internalized storytelling voice? How has it changed or stayed the same?

Spinning stories through my head is a lifetime habit of mine. I think many of us tell ourselves stories in one form or another, as a way of giving meaning to what is happening to us and around us. The fear of adult ridicule was why, as a child, I began to keep my stories to myself. Now, rather than going around talking out loud to myself, I write the stories down.

2. You repeatedly describe the schoolhouse as a time capsule, and by definition, time capsules hold items that were familiar to one generation (insiders) but become mysterious to a much later generation (outsiders). When writing about secrets in nonfiction, in what ways does the author have to be both an insider and an outsider to the secret?

The time capsule holds objects that are familiar to me and yet hold secrets of their own: why this particular school reader, lying open-faced on a dusty floor? Whose hands last turned its pages? Why has this one-room schoolhouse, even derelict, survived when so many have not? The nonfiction writer searches the time capsule for clues like a detective in a crowd of criminals and then describes for her readers what she knows and what she suspects.

3. What truth were you able to expose in the nonfiction version that you were unable to expose in the fiction version of the narrative and/or vice versa?

In my fictional version of what happened at the Duck Creek School, I could hide behind the mask of my character by giving him motives and desires that were not my own. In nonfiction, the mask is always more subtle: the reader must believe in the writer. The reader who believes that the writer is withholding the truth about herself or lying about herself is a reader who will stop trusting the writer.

4. It might be strange for today's readers to understand how anyone kept silent about Mrs. Skaarda's unprofessional behavior at the time it was happening. Would you mind discussing this silence in a bit more detail? What cultural shifts have you seen that might speak to the lack of student

and parent silence today? Do these cultural shifts change anything for nonfiction writers?

Mrs. Skaarda, as I call her, was the wife of a respected rancher in a small and close-knit rural community. As a teacher, she was trusted, which in a time when parents complain to school boards about the grades their children are getting may seem strange. But those were the days, after all, when children were told that if they ever got a licking at school, they'd get another when they got home. Fiction writers and nonfiction writers must show their readers what matters in the worlds they are depicting. It's always a balancing act—have I explained too much? Too little?

On Lying

Sarah Gorham

I CONFESS. I EXCUSED MY DAUGHTER'S ABSENCE FROM SCHOOL WITH A LIE. WE wanted to get a jump on our vacation, so I told Sister Paulette that Bonnie would be attending her great-uncle Max's funeral on Friday. Indeed, he had passed away last winter, the touch of truth that made the lie easier. It takes some chutzpa to lie to a nun, though people of all ages have been doing it for years.

What did I feel? About twelve years old, like one of the girls roaming around me in their hiked-up blue skirts.

But I was determined, with a specific purpose in mind: we would leave early for the long drive to Door County, avoiding late afternoon traffic. Bonnie's commitment to her classes and Sister Paulette were the only obstacles. My lie, like most lies, was a method of achieving my goal. Our goal, my family's goal, that of expediency or safety or however I justified it at the time.

I was also careful, perhaps more so than the uniformed teenagers around me. After all, I was replacing the truth with a falsehood and it had to be believable, with characters, details, motivations. Believable, but simple; I couldn't imagine myself reciting an elaborate story, sustaining that kind of false energy.

"Liars should have good memories." (proverb)

Later, well-rested and back in my routine of dropping Bonnie off at school, seeing her safely inside, then leaving for work, Sister Paulette pulled me aside. We sat together under the bronze crucifix and sentimental portrait of Our Savior, the office a whirlwind of bells, buzzers, and flicked ponytails. I wondered if the school was bankrupt and she was breaking the news to each parent individually. Or maybe Bonnie was in trouble of some kind. I was alert and confused. Sister Paulette held my hands in hers and peered directly into my pupils, as if to check for shrinkage. She whispered, "I'm so sorry for your loss."

Loss. My chin dropped. I glanced to the left, hoping to recover my bearings, felt a pilot light catch under my skin and heat climb. I had forgotten all about the long-suffering uncle. My response came after a long pause, during which time I was frantically searching my backup files. "Sorry for your loss," I repeated. "Oh, that loss. Well, he was a distant uncle. We were not very close to him."

Sister Paulette saw it all. If she hadn't been 100 percent confident before, she must have noticed my relief when the subject changed, and we began to discuss the air-conditioned county in Wisconsin where we relaxed and recreated. If I had been telling the truth, I might have been a bit more eager to return to the theme. A woman who has lost someone wears her grief like a plus-size coat: her skin droops, her shoulders slide. I was refreshed after my two-weeks-and-a-day vacation and rather perky.

The body never lies. In its collusion with the truth, it avoids eye contact, limits movement of arms and hands. The liar is not likely to touch her chest, but fidgets a lot, grazing face, throat, hair. She backs up in her chair, sits stiffly, compresses her physical space. Timing and duration of emotional gestures are also slightly off—too short or late. When a liar is faking emotion—delight or grief—her facial expressions can't really get into it. Eyebrows furrow as if a fly were in the air; a smile's confined to the lips instead of the whole face.

Aphasics, who have lost the ability to speak or understand language, quickly develop an acute sensitivity to physical gesture. They are among the best lie detectors, reports Nancy L. Etcoff, and others, in *Nature* magazine. They pick up all their clues from watching a liar move, rather than listening to her speech.

My mother too was gifted with an unusually keen social intelligence, or "shit detector," as she called it. She distrusted Phil Donahue, and Gordon Liddy *before* the Watergate scandal broke. Though Lutheran by baptism, she had a Jewish impatience with niceties, euphemisms, whitewashing, and could see from a mile away whether someone was faking it.

This made my adolescence difficult. To honor my curfew, I went to bed at eleven, locked my door, climbed onto a chair under the window, cranked the handle, squeezed through, and dropped to the begonias below. Then I'd walk briskly to the bridge by Mohegan and Goldsboro, where my boyfriend stood smoking under haloed streetlights. Night after night after night, our relationship secretly flourished.

Weeding the side yard one hot afternoon, my mother spotted the crushed flowers. I blurted out an explanation: *It must have been those dogs. A whole pack of them. Look what they've done!* We both knew the real story. To my mother, it wasn't worth the fight, so nothing surfaced, little changed, except perhaps my avoidance of her begonias when I leapt into the steamy dark.

In common use from the fourteenth all the way up to the seventeenth century was the adjective *gull*, of Germanic origin, which meant "yellow or pale." The noun *gull* referred to "an unfledged bird, especially a gosling." A young, inexperienced bird, pale and yellow, might be easily deceived. From this comes the word "gullible."

Though pale, Sister Paulette was no fledgling bird, sparrow, or goose. Neither was my mother.

"Kindness should override truth." (Samuel Butler)

I don't think my parents ever lied to me. No, I take it back. The worst I remember is a kind of imprecision. When asked about the results of my IQ test, she responded, "Oh, somewhere between mine and your father's." I could tell, in the name of tenderness, she allowed herself a white lie, a clean cloth over a knotty table. I was satisfied with her answer and sat like a sparrow, safe between my parents on the swaying intelligence wire.

The truth is often too hurtful, terrifying, unpleasant, mundane, or confusing to deal with. It begs embellishment. As a consequence, in varying degrees, for multiple reasons lying is an essential element of social interaction. Here are four points on a possibly infinite list of examples:

- Joni Mitchell doesn't wear makeup: "Not really. . . . a little blush, concealer, a dash of mascara, a little color on the lips. And that's it." Joni wants us to think her beauty is effortless. The *Times* calls this "make-up denial."
- Please do not call them McMansions. They are *luxury estates*, a phrase that conjures up Versailles, Fontainebleau, Kensington Gardens in the shade-dappled, rolling hills of England or France. For a mere 5 or 6 million, you too can be a count, lord and lady, prince or princess from a long line of blue bloods.
- The director promises to get you started in the very next play, scheduled for spring. When you don't sleep with him, the part never materializes; you can't even get him on the phone.
- "I did not have sexual relations with that woman," said President Clinton. Note his avoidance of the contraction "didn't," his formalizing, distancing himself from Monica Lewinsky. Thousands of teenagers are now "abstaining from sex" by practicing fellatio. This benefits boys in particular, a happy new population of Little Bills.

A lie is a social tool. We lie to avoid consequences—hurting the feelings of a loved one, embarrassment, a "time-out," failure, impeachment, jail, or sometimes just because it's easier than relaying the complicated truth (I borrowed the sweater from my sister who borrowed it from her roommate who bought it at a thrift shop. Or: Thank you. I don't remember where I got it.) We also lie to get something we want, whether it is a fluffier version of our lackluster selves, a longer vacation, membership in some elite intellectual group, or a house in the Pacific Palisades.

Even animals will lie. Our hound dog Emma sleeps on the living room couch; it's her spot, her kingdom. When her sibling Monty hops up there before her, she rushes to the front door to let roll her mellifluous, hound-dog bellow. There is, of course, no intruder. We all know she's faking, except Monty, who jumps off the couch to join in the fray. Who can blame him? It's the wolf's cry, the irresistible bugle call of the hunt. He's bewitched, and falls for it every time. As soon as he lands on all fours, Emma stops barking abruptly and leaps onto the couch before Monty knows what hit him.

There are some cases where lying is *a virtue* in the animal kingdom. Consider the nesting plover who spots a predator and immediately begins an elaborate charade of limping, squealing, dragging, and dipping of one supposedly broken wing towards an adjacent sand dune and away from her brood. Animals dissemble for many of the same reasons we do. Monty's hair rises along his spine and he grows two inches taller. A magnificent frigate bird puffs up its scarlet feathers until its throat is bigger than a bear's heart. Plants too: The mountain laurel's pollen-coated, spring-loaded stamens are painted a bright, alluring pink. From scent and color, the lady slipper creates a tantalizing canoe-shaped trap for bees and spiders.

Rocks and cement do not lie. The very idea is absurd. It appears the lie is a characteristic of *living* things, an extension of Darwinian notions of natural selection. The liar, whether plant or animal, casts a spell for a handful of reasons: to jump-start the reproductive process, protect their young, defend their territory, escape predation, scare or intimidate rivals, or otherwise appear more fit in the world's eye.

> *"The most enchanting things in nature and art are based on deception."*
> (Vladimir Nabokov)

Here is a poem that describes a deception gone wild, from Jeffrey Harrison's collection *Feeding the Fire*:

OUR OTHER SISTER

The cruelest thing I did to my younger sister
wasn't shooting a homemade blowdart into her knee,
where it dangled for a breathless second

before dropping off, but telling her we had
another, older sister who'd gone away.
What my motives were I can't recall: a whim,

or was it some need of mine to toy with loss,
to probe the ache of imaginary wounds?
But that first sentence was like a string of DNA

that replicated itself in coiling lies
when my sister began asking her desperate questions.
I called our older sister Isabel

and gave her hazel eyes and long blonde hair.
I had her run away to California
where she took drugs and made hippie jewelry.

Before I knew it, she'd moved to Santa Fe
and opened a shop. She sent a postcard
every year or so, but she'd stopped calling.

I can still see my younger sister staring at me,
her eyes widening with desolation
then filling with tears. I can still remember

how thrilled and horrified I was
that something I'd just made up
had that kind of power, and I can just feel

the blowdart of remorse stabbing me in the heart
as I rushed to tell her none of it was true.
But it was too late. Our other sister

had already taken shape, and we could not
call her back from her life far away
or tell her how badly we missed her.

The first false sentence the speaker recalls in this poem—the pronouncement and vague shape of another sister—is the easiest. But a lie is seldom solitary; it begs another and another, until an imaginary skeleton is built, bone by bone, muscle and flesh, a sister-hologram with hobbies, home, hair. The greater the detail, the less likely she will crumble. The longer her history, the greater the strain, until he can't even make the truth believable, and must suffer "the blowdart of remorse."

Initially, the speaker lies to get what he wants. Perhaps it began with a whim.

Or big-brother meanness, like the homemade blowdart. Perhaps indeed the speaker was "toying with loss," or "prob[ing] the ache of imaginary wounds." Whatever the motivation, the lie flatters the liar. Like Joni Mitchell's "make-up denial," or the frigate bird's magnificent feathers, it allows him "that kind of power."

True consciousness, the recognition of self separated from world, occurs at around age seven, the age at which a child also begins to lie. Teenagers are notorious liars. They lie about their whereabouts, drugs and alcohol, school attendance, grades, boyfriends, sex, mostly to avoid punishment from various authority figures. But they lie to their friends as well, boosting their intelligence, sexual experience, *cool* quotient. The high social pressure of adolescence makes them desperate for any and every kind of "spell." It is often a way of *being*. Bonnie once told her teacher she had been abused and now her parents were divorcing. She noticed how victims were getting all the attention, their status clearly elevated to the point of celebrity. Again, we were pulled into the Sister's office as the first step in a kind of intervention. We could see the open training manual on her desk, as well as a xeroxed list of professional counselors.

Perhaps lying follows the natural curve of a child's independence—my lie makes me NOT YOU. My lie makes me ME. Human beings are not ants who, lifelong, remain committed to their basic job description. We have the ability to depart from communal dependence. The lie, whether to avoid or get something, is the primitive beginning of the effort to distinguish oneself.

Like most young people, I experimented with a variety of personas, from Amazonian firefighter to urban botanist to country schoolteacher. Only the poet stuck, but even then, in order to write poems, I faked masculinity. I dressed in jeans and a flannel shirt, sat at a table swept clean of comforting objects. Then I imagined how a guy would see the mule grazing in my front yard, the piles of rotten osage oranges, dirt road winding out to our mailbox, and grackles decimating the few tomatoes left in our garden. I feigned confidence. My voice deepened and I began to write, using description as a way in.

Back then, this maleness was where most of the published works came from, where the good ideas lived, or so it seemed. My poems had almost nothing to do with my true life; they were chill, disembodied fabrications. But I believed in them, and they were successful, published in prestigious literary magazines.

Not long after, I married and had a baby, a colicky no-sleeper whose very existence squashed my conceit like an egg carton. Pretend to be a man when your entire body is in service to a famished child, *a female* at her functional peak? After three years of this, I hardly recognized the person who had written my poems. It was absurd, even impossible to lie, to play the cowboy again and pick up where I left off. I began a slow crawl back to some semblance of honesty in my work, and then to publish these poems at the level I had before. Now I partition off my identity, using my maiden or "professional" name for poems and essays, my married name for church newsletters and legal documents, and a little bit of both for my work in publishing. This fits right in with shifting notions of the "self." We are made of *many* selves, not just one. Over a lifetime, we float between honesty and fabrication, between conformity—our dependence on others—and the urge to be separate from them. Maybe the natural truth *is* dependence and the denial of it necessary for us to accomplish anything beyond basic survival.

In Harrison's poem the speaker lies to his sister, his incentive a whim or cruelty or the need to appear larger than life, like the magnificent frigate bird. But what of the poem itself? Is the writer telling the truth? Was there a sister at all, trusting and loyal? If not, what are the writer's motives in deceiving us? What can we make of this enchantment inside an enchantment, writing that casts a spell on the reader too?

The con man may employ wit and cleverness in his scam, but his lie remains a "poor man's lie," with close ties to evolutionary pressure. His enchantment is basic and blunt. Freud would place the artist only slightly above the criminal. In his assessment "[the artist] desires to win honor, power, wealth, fame and the love of women."

But art is not solely a form of greed and self-aggrandizement. Harrison's poem, by the nature of its medium, will never bring him more than a few dollars. At best, a successful poem will garner a thousand extra readers, hardly the legions of adoring fans that flock to rock concerts. Doesn't the artist also compose a suite of songs to remember, or reactivate some past music in herself? Paint to safeguard the view from a farmhouse window, visualize a betrayal, pleasure, loss? Write to understand, clarify, generalize, move from the micro to the macro, the personal to the public, like a set of Russian dolls, opened in reverse?

Artists play with reality, whether they manipulate language, paint, or a digital camera. Call it poetic license, embellishment, or outright lying, they are loose in their allegiance to facts. How interesting that the word *fact* comes from the Latin *factum*, to do or make. It's the same root for *artifice, counterfeit, façade, facsimile*. Icarus's wings did not melt when he defied the warning and flew close to the sun. A princess cannot really feel a pea under dozens of mattresses. Artists prevaricate in order to tell the truth.

Here's another poem (mine), rife with deception:

HOMESICKNESS

On another continent, mother circles the farmhouse.
She steams gnocchi, tosses them in butter.

Mother and daughter have matching teeth, like a zipper.

If daughter flies home she'll lose eight hours. If her car were amphibious,
the loss would be hardly perceptible.

There's always the mail. And the cell phone, like a human cowbell.
Especially if you are loved.

Mother rings her from the bus stop, train station, grocery store.
When it's time to pay, she says hang on. The bus pulls up, gotta go, so long!

Emotion: from the Latin *emovere*—to move away, "in transport."

How would a jet land in the country, gravel roads
and all those electric fences?

She opens her mail, a blue mountain of *Mit Luftpost, Par Avion*.

Genes are a kind of blue letter from a mother
to her daughter: Good news, bad news.

What is a mother but a tooth's way of producing another tooth?

My mother never lived in a farmhouse; she was raised in suburban Milwaukee. My mother and I do not have matching teeth, like a zipper. The zipper came first as an image of connection/disconnection; our teeth match only in the sense that all teeth match, although I had braces and she did not. It is not true my mother rings me on the fly; in fact, cell phones did not exist during her lifetime. "What is a mother," I conclude, "but a tooth's way of producing another tooth?" This is a rather cold statement stumbled upon by fusing genetic "blue letters" and those matching teeth—a drastic reduction of a mother's role, true to the poem, true perhaps of some mothers, but definitely not true of mine.

Asked about the origins of poetry, Nabokov responded, "When a cave boy came running back to the cave, through the tall grass, shouting as he ran, 'Wolf, wolf,' and there *was* no wolf, his baboon-like parents, great sticklers for the truth, gave him a hiding, no doubt, but poetry had been born—the tall story had been born in the tall grass." Tall tales, yarns, fish stories—there are many names for this sort of lie. But in most cases, the motives are similar: to entertain *yes*, but also to get at a truth the facts won't allow. Perhaps lying has, by its narrow definition, been given a bad name. Maybe *Ulysses* is an elaborate lie, originating on the same ground as the Mafia don denying the assassination of an entire family. The difference is complexity and, of course, motivation. The Mafioso's lie is simple survival. The lying artist hints at a deeper definition of self and a greater organization of world. My lie to the nun was pure greed and selfish desire.

Sister Paulette wore an indigo habit of the modern style, skirt just below the knee, sensible shoes. She was sturdy and moved nimbly for someone her age. I couldn't help but notice she'd sprung for the more expensive graduated lenses for her wire-rimmed glasses. After years spent absorbing and dodging various crises, demands, and fibs, she was a solid combination of common sense, spiritual discipline, and perhaps the slightest hint of vanity.

Or, there were no graduated lenses, no sensible shoes, indeed, no Paulette or Catholic school named Sacred Heart. Like Harrison, I have designed a Sister-hologram with language and imagination, instead of bone and blood—all inventions to dramatize the story, to underscore the flagrancy of a lie and its uncomfortable consequences. Perhaps Bonnie went to a huge public school with an overworked staff and a multitude of misbehaving students. Perhaps we picked her up as usual on Thursday and hit the road early the next morning. Her absence on Friday would hardly have been noticed. It doesn't really matter. I'm almost not sure myself after all these years—a lifetime of truths, lies, truths that turned out to be lies, lies that turned out to be true. It's all part of the effort to explain what I'm doing here, on earth.

Interview with Sarah Gorham

1. Your opening lines strike a conversational tone, as if the reader is a trusted friend. Can you point to other parts of the essay where you reach out to the reader this way? When writing the truth about lies, why is it essential to treat the reader as a confidante?

We should open an essay with something arresting, the equivalent of catching the reader's eye across a table or, as I imagine, physically drawing the reader aside by her sleeve. Look, I'm willing to tell you a secret and believe me it's worth your attention. Furthermore, you are the only one worth talking to. It's flattering to the reader, it pares away the usual small talk, and the tone suggests this will really be *something*. Who could resist?

What happens after that is anyone's guess. We are casting a spell—owning up to a small lie could lead the way to a no-holds-barred confession or a greater deception. I use research to bring in the world—how a lie effects a liar's physiognomy, how animals prevaricate, how celebrities stretch the truth—but also to reassure the reader. I also check in with other confidences: I include not just Jeffrey Harrison's "Our Other Sister," a poem about a self-perpetuating lie, but my own "Homesickness," a way to deepen the trust: *I wouldn't share this with just anyone: I lied about my mother.*

We can be trustworthy and tell only the truth, or we can play with that trust, which in my mind is a lot more interesting.

2. You bring up the body language of liars, which is fascinating. Do you think there is a parallel "writing language" of honesty and of lying? For example, when you are reading an essay or memoir that just seems too good to be true, what clues you in that this writer is really telling the truth (or not)?

Here's where the cliché applies: the devil's in the details (or the lack thereof). It's pretty easy to tell when a hike along the south face of Mount Everest is fabricated, because the writer backs off from the up-close sensual minutiae and gives us something generic instead. Anyone can muster *that* from a photograph. We can also borrow from someone else's narrative if we so choose, and that is yet another way to lie. But if the writer has *been there*, absorbing the scene with all her senses, her obsessions and oddities, her path along the ridge is a very particular one. And it feels true because of this.

The eyes shift, her fingers flit about, facial expressions "can't really get into it": a lying body avoids and therefore loses its focus. A writer must have an intimate, knowledgeable engagement with a subject. Otherwise, the language will be vague or just plain phony. If a writer strongly believes and convinces us her rendering is closer to the truth, it's really hard to tell it's *not* the truth.

3. You make the point that lying is a tool in small talk and conversation, especially useful if we know we don't need to be "relaying the complicated truth." Writers of creative nonfiction often decide to leave out facts for this reason. It's not the same as lying, of course, but it's also not the full truth. What advice do you have for beginning writers who are bogged down in telling the complicated truth, yet they are also worried about the ethics of cutting too much or glossing over facts?

It's best to home in on one small incident, the very one that sticks in your mind after years have passed. What you're doing is no different from memory itself, which edits out most of a life. If you remember an event clearly, it's bound to contain visuals, snippets of dialogue, emotional salience. It also gives you a place to begin. So important! Don't feel like you must honor the facts unless you plan to turn the essay into a textbook for ultrasound technicians. Not at this point. You are shaping this incident for the reader so she too can see what you saw, feel what you felt.

"On Lying" began with the last scene in Sister Pauline's office. Because my embarrassment was so acute and difficult to forget, much of the scene was easy to re-create without too much embellishment. But I left a lot out. I discarded the footsteps that led me to her office, the other nuns in the room. Believe me, you're not missing anything. I even dropped Bonnie's reaction to my lie, if she was even present. I no longer remember.

4. Will you share with us how you decided on the end of your essay? And do you ever get comments from readers about that twist at the end?

I rarely read this essay out loud because it's longer than the others and comments from readers have mostly addressed the book as a whole. But one friend of mine laughed nervously and said the last two paragraphs really shook him up. It was the reaction I hoped for, though I'm trying this reader's trust of my work and me. I certainly don't want him taking me less seriously. Some truths are indisputable: the earth revolves on its axis, tides are linked to the moon, water will boil when it reaches a certain temperature. But so many other truths fall apart under scrutiny, evolving and devolving over time. I liked the idea of beginning the essay in medias res, with a specific lie. Then ending it up in the air, casting a shadow over everything that came before.

Contributors' Notes

Samuel Autman is a member of DePauw University's writing faculty in Green-castle, Indiana. His essay "Invisible Nails" won first place in the SLS-Disquiet 2015 Literary Contest in nonfiction and was published in the *Ninth Letter* literary magazine. "A Dash of Pepper in the Snow" appears in *The Chalk Circle: Prizewinning Intercultural Essays* anthology. His other essays have appeared in *Black Gay Genius: Answering Joseph Beam's Call*, the *Common Reader*, *Under the Gum Tree*, *Brevity: A Journal of Concise Literary Nonfiction*, the *Huffington Post* and the *Good Men Project*. He is currently at work on *Sanctified: A Memoir*.

Jo Ann Beard is an essayist and creative nonfiction writer. She is the author of the novel *In Zanesville* and *The Boys of My Youth*, a collection of autobiographical essays, as well as essays/articles published in magazines, journals, and anthologies. She received a Whiting Writers' Award and a Guggenheim Fellowship.

Mary Clearman Blew recently retired from the University of Idaho, where she taught in the MFA program in creative writing. Her short fiction collection, *Runaway*, won a Pacific Northwest Booksellers Award, as did her memoir *All*

But the Waltz: Essays on a Montana Family. A novel, *Jackalope Dreams*, won the Western Heritage Award. Her most recent book is *This Is Not the Ivy League: A Memoir.*

Jill Christman is the author of *Darkroom: A Family Exposure* (AWP Award Series in Creative Nonfiction winner), *Borrowed Babies: Apprenticing for Motherhood*, and essays in magazines and journals such as *Brevity, Fourth Genre, Iron Horse Literary Review, Literary Mama, Oprah Magazine, River Teeth, Brain, Child, Phoebe,* and *TriQuarterly.* She serves on the board of the Association of Writers and Writing Programs (AWP) and teaches creative nonfiction writing in Ashland University's low-residency MFA program and at Ball State University in Muncie, Indiana, where she lives with her husband, writer Mark Neely, and their two children.

Kelly Kathleen Ferguson is the author of *My Life as Laura: How I Searched for Laura Ingalls Wilder and Found Myself.* Her work has appeared in *Witness, New England Review, mental_floss magazine, Storysouth,* and *McSweeney's Internet Tendency*, among other publications. She is an Assistant Professor of Language and Literature at Southern Utah University.

Sarah Gorham is a poet and essayist and most recently the author of *Study in Perfect*, selected by Bernard Cooper for the 2013 AWP Award in Creative Nonfiction, and the book-length essay *Alpine Apprentice.* Gorham is also the author of four collections of poetry—*Bad Daughter, The Cure, The Tension Zone,* and *Don't Go Back to Sleep.* Other honors include grants and fellowships from the National Endowment for the Arts and three state arts councils. She is cofounder and editor-in-chief at Sarabande Books.

Robin Hemley is the winner of a Guggenheim Fellowship and many other awards, including the Nelson Algren Award for Fiction from the *Chicago Tribune*, and three Pushcart Prizes in both fiction and nonfiction. He has published eleven books, and his stories and essays have appeared in the *New York Times, New York Magazine, Chicago Tribune*, and many literary magazines and anthologies. Robin received his MFA from the Iowa Writers' Workshop and directed the Nonfiction Writing Program at the University of Iowa for nine years. He is currently Writer-in-Residence and Director of the Writing Program at Yale-NUS in Singapore.

Jen Hirt's memoir, *Under Glass: The Girl with a Thousand Christmas Trees*, won the Drake University Emerging Writer Award. Her essay "Lores of Last Unicorns," published in the *Gettysburg Review*, won a Pushcart Prize. She is the coeditor with Erin Murphy of *Creating Nonfiction: Twenty Essays and Interviews with the Writers*. Her essays have also received the Gabehart Prize for Nonfiction from the Kentucky Women Writers Conference, a Pennsylvania Council on the Arts grant, and three notable essay mentions in *Best American Essays*. She is an Assistant Professor of Creative Writing at Penn State Harrisburg.

Leslie Jamison is the author of *The Empathy Exams*, a New York Times bestselling essay collection, and a novel, *The Gin Closet*, a finalist for the Los Angeles Times First Fiction Award. Her work has appeared in *Harper's, Oxford American, A Public Space, Boston Review, Virginia Quarterly Review, The Believer*, and the *New York Times*, where she is a regular columnist for the Sunday Book Review. She lives in Brooklyn and is an Assistant Professor at Columbia University.

Brenda Miller teaches in the MFA in Creative Writing program and the MA in English Studies at Western Washington University. She is the author of five essay collections, including *An Earlier Life, Listening Against the Stone*, and *Season of the Body*. She also coauthored *Tell It Slant: Creating, Refining and Publishing Creative Nonfiction* and *The Pen and the Bell: Mindful Writing in a Busy World*. Her work has received six Pushcart Prizes.

Tina Mitchell earned her MFA at the University of Idaho and her PhD at the University of Louisiana at Lafayette. She is a cofounder of *Rougarou* and *im-possible* and the founding editor of *The Turnip Truck(s)*. She is currently an Adjunct Instructor at UL Lafayette.

Erin Murphy is the author of six collections of poetry, most recently *Ancilla*, which was the winner of the Womack Book Award. She has twice won the Paterson Prize for Literary Excellence. With Todd Davis, she is the coeditor of *Making Poems: Forty Poems with Commentary by the Poets*, and with Jen Hirt she is the coeditor of *Creating Nonfiction: Twenty Essays and Interviews with the Writers*. She is Professor of English and Creative Writing at Penn State Altoona.

Jon Pineda is the author of the memoir *Sleep in Me*, a Barnes & Noble Discover Great New Writers selection and a *Library Journal* "Best Books of 2010" selection. His novel *Apology* won the Milkweed National Fiction Prize. His poetry collections are *Little Anodynes*, selected by Nikky Finney for the Palmetto Poetry Series, *The Translator's Diary*, winner of the Green Rose Prize from New Issues, and *Birthmark*, selected by Ralph Burns as winner of the Crab Orchard Award Series in Poetry Open Competition. He lives in Virginia and teaches at the University of Mary Washington.

Amy E. Robillard is Professor of English at Illinois State University, where she teaches graduate and undergraduate courses in the personal essay, rhetorical theory, composition theory, authorship theory, and life writing. She is the coeditor, with Ron Fortune, of *Authorship Contested: Cultural Challenges to the Authentic, Autonomous Author*, and her work has been published in a number of academic journals. Her personal essays can be found on *Full Grown People* and *The Rumpus*. In everything she writes, she aims to contest the artificial boundaries between the academic and the personal.

Barrett Swanson is the 2016–2017 Halls Emerging Artist Fellow at the Wisconsin Institute for Creative Writing. He is a recipient of a Pushcart Prize, and his short fiction and essays have been distinguished as "notable" in the *Best American Nonrequired Reading* and the *Best American Essays*. His work has appeared most recently in the *New Republic, American Short Fiction, The Point, Mississippi Review, Ninth Letter*, and *Boston Review*.

Ron Tanner's awards for writing include a Faulkner Society gold medal, a Pushcart Prize, a New Letters Award, a Best of the Web Award, a Maryland Arts Council grant, and many others. He is the author of four books, most recently *Missile Paradise*, a novel. He teaches writing at Loyola University-Maryland and directs the Marshall Islands Story Project.

Acknowledgments

Samuel Autman, "Invisible Nails," first appeared in *Ninth Letter* as an online Special Feature: Featured Writer #54 (Summer 2015). Reprinted by permission of the author. Copyright 2015 by Samuel Autman.

Jo Ann Beard, "Maybe It Happened," first appeared in *O, the Oprah Magazine* (August 2008). Reprinted by permission of *O, the Oprah Magazine/Hearst Publications* and the author. Copyright 2015 by Jo Ann Beard.

Mary Clearman Blew, "Leaving Duck Creek," first appeared in the *Georgia Review*, vol. 66, no. 1 (Spring 2012), where it was paired with the fiction version, "Forby and the Mayan Maidens." Reprinted by permission of the author. Copyright 2015 by Mary Clearman Blew.

Jill Christman, "Three Takes on a Jump," first appeared in *Partly True*, a special online issue of the *Mississippi Review* in Summer 2007. Reprinted by permission of the author. Copyright 2006 by Jill Christman.

Kelly Kathleen Ferguson, "Experiments in Living Chemistry," first appeared in *Witness*, vol. 25, no. 3 (Fall 2012). Reprinted by permission of the author. Copyright 2015 by Kelly Kathleen Ferguson.

Sarah Gorham, "On Lying," first appeared in *Quarterly West*, no. 64 (Spring/ Summer 2007) and in *Study in Perfect* (University of Georgia Press, 2014). Reprinted by permission of the University of Georgia Press and the author. Copyright 2015 by Sarah Gorham.

Jeffrey Harrison, "Our Other Sister," first appeared in the *Southern Review* and was collected in *Feeding the Fire* (Sarabande Books, 2001). This poem appears in full in this book in "On Lying" by Sarah Gorham. Reprinted by permission of the author. Copyright 2015 by Jeffrey Harrison.

Robin Hemley, "Reading History to My Mother," first appeared in *Fourth Genre*, vol. 1, no. 1 (Spring 1999). Reprinted by permission of the author. Copyright 2015 by Robin Hemley.

Jen Hirt, "Not Less Than 1,000 Bottles for Horseradish," first appeared in *Ninth Letter*, vol. 11, no. 1 (Spring/Summer 2014). Reprinted by permission of the author. Copyright 2015 by Jen Hirt.

Leslie Jamison, "The Empathy Exams," from *The Empathy Exams: Essays*. Copyright © 2014 by Leslie Jamison. Reprinted with the permission of The Permissions Company, Inc., on behalf of Graywolf Press, www.graywolfpress.org.

Brenda Miller, "Secret Machine," first appeared in *Agni Online* (2008). Reprinted by permission of the author. Copyright 2015 by Brenda Miller.

Tina Mitchell, "Dog Psychology." Copyright 2016 by Tina Mitchell.

Erin Murphy, "White Lies," first appeared in *Brevity*, July 11, 2010. Reprinted by permission of the author. Copyright 2015 by Erin Murphy.

Jon Pineda, "S-Turns." Copyright 2015 by Jon Pineda.

Amy E. Robillard, "Changing the Subject," first appeared in *The Rumpus*, May 27, 2015. Reprinted by permission of the author. Copyright 2015 by Amy E. Robillard.

Barrett Swanson, "Okay Forever," first appeared in an earlier version as "This Swift and Violent Forgetting" in *Ninth Letter*, vol. 11, no. 1 (Spring/Summer 2014). Reprinted by permission of the author. Copyright 2015 by Barrett Swanson.

Ron Tanner, "My Father's Secrets," first appeared in *Creative Nonfiction: The Memoir Issue*, no. 55 (Spring 2015). Reprinted by permission of the author. Copyright 2015 by Ron Tanner.

Our sincere thanks to Megan Conrad, our editorial assistant in the early stages of this publication.